RIBA BUILDING INDUSTRY TRUST

The RIBA Building Industry Trust is sponsored by a group of well known companies drawn from different sectors of the building industry. The current companies are:

British Alcan Aluminium Limited
ICI Paints Division Dulux Trade Group
Formica Limited
Ideal-Standard Limited
London Brick Company Limited
Marley Roof Tile Company Limited
G & S Allgood Limited
SMP (Group) Limited

Its principle objective is to promote the relationship between the Royal Institute of British Architects and the Building Industry.

Architecture and the Higher Learning

The Design Studio
An Exploration of its Traditions and Potentials

RIBA Publications Limited
for
RIBA Building Industry Trust

© 1985
Donald Schon/MIT
and
RIBA Building Industry Trust
66 Portland Place
London W1A 4AD
England

Published
by
RIBA Publications Limited
Finsbury Mission, Moreland Street, London EC1V 8VB

Printed
by
Frank Peters (Printers) Ltd,
Kendal, Cumbria, England.

ISBN 0 947877 45 2

Preface

This study was commissioned by the RIBA Industry Trust as a contribution to the 'great education debate' of the 1980's, a debate concerned both with general education and that of architects in particular.

Architecture and design teaching methods are being seen increasingly as models for avoiding the polarisation of the arts and the sciences in traditional secondary education; an 'education to some purpose' involving both intellectual and practical ability. Such an education produces young people with a much greater all round capability, of great value to them and society. Such people are also just the kind that a diverse industry such as building needs in all its many facets.

It is hoped that Dr. Schon's work will also aid 'The Education for Capability' campaign of the Royal Society of Arts.

Keith Ingham
Chairman
RIBA Building Industry Trust.

Foreword

by
Professor David Gosling

Professor Schon has recognised the renewed interest in
architectural education internationally. Perhaps because
architecture has become a fashionable vocation, similar in
appeal to law and medicine, the current view may be that there
are too many people crowding the profession. This is certainly
a view held at the time by the Government of the United
Kingdom and members of the Royal Institute of British
Architects, both bodies wishing to see a drastic reduction in
numbers. Inevitably, such a view encourages a reappraisal of
architectural education with the intention not only of
encouraging fewer students to enter schools of architecture but
acting as a challenge concerning the very validity of
architectural education in its present form. It is certainly true
that, before politically imposed pressures on architectural
education occurred, the status of architectural schools within
the higher educational system was uneasy in not satisfying the
more obvious criteria which may be applied to science and
engineering; for example, the level of research funding,
presentation of papers at international conferences or the
quality of published work for learned societies. Quality of
design achievement either on the part of teacher or student is
considered largely irrelevant in the harsh reality of academic
competition in universities.

To suggest, therefore, that other professions taught in
institutions of higher learning have much to learn from
architectural education is a radical, if not unique, point of view.

Donald Schon rightly points to the architectural studio as a
quite special form of education in the creative arts, drawing
upon precedent in the craft system of the medieval guilds as
well as the 19th century École des Beaux Arts. The greatest of

the European architects in the early part of this century used the atelier system and this influenced strongly the organisation of schools of architecture both in Europe and North America. It is also true that studio work in schools of architecture sometimes bears little resemblance to conventional architectural practice of today, particularly with regard to what Donald Schon describes as "the laborious rendering of technical detail". The advocates of computer-aided design in architecture would argue that it is precisely by the extensive utilisation of computers that the need for laborious technical details could be obviated and that the creative aspects of the architectural studio would then be more closely reflected in practice.

This book interestingly draws comparisons between the architectural profession and its use of design "language" and parallels in other professions such as law and medicine. It has been argued elsewhere, however, that "learning-by-doing" in architecture draws upon the experience of medical teaching rather than vice versa. Attempts have been made in the United Kingdom to introduce the idea of the teaching practice in architectural education in the same way that upper year medical students are assigned to hospital wards under the guidance of medical professors, using techniques of problem solving in their route towards medical qualification. Without the impressive resources of the National Health Service, however, it is unlikely that such experiments in architecture would succeed at present and though building pathology has latterly become a new specialism in architectural education, the comprehensive study of building failures as the essence and core of teaching might be questionable. There is an argument for a process of reflection rather than precipitate action in the studio system of teaching in an attempt to demistify the intuitive approaches to criticism.

Professor Schon's detailed account and case study of studio presentation by an individual student makes fascinating reading; with each design review described graphically. Such an analysis is of great interest to any architectural teacher in assessing comparative processes in other schools of architecture. There is a persistent emphasis on spatial relationships in which the particular student in the case-study and her teacher seem to reject some functional requirements of cost and program which normally occur in architectural practice. Donald Schon acknowledges this in accepting that designers might differ with respect to the priorities they assign to "design domains".

There is a further problem which the book emphasises. Contrary to the doctrine of architectural education a decade or more ago, architectural design now comprises an extremely complex pluralist approach with the danger of the architect becoming merely a designer of façades and styles, as in the 19th century, and contribute little to real design development by the end of the present century. It is suggested that the analysis of design evaluation described provides an independence from stylistic considerations. That is to say, such an evaluation, based upon a form of objectivity, allows the architect to fulfill new and more demanding roles such as architect-developer. New roles require an even wider base of knowledge and it is difficult to see how these new fields of knowledge can be taught within the conventional system of architectural education. It is also suggested here that there could be a possibility of architectural education incorporating units of research-based theory and technique while retaining the traditions of the studio as the heat of the curriculum. Professor Schon cites two examples in this book — at the University of Southern California concerning solar research and at Harvard Graduate School of Design concerning the interaction of urban design. Yet generally, the situation of the medical students in the clinic, the engineers in the laboratory or the social workers in the field, does not yet apply in architecture. The proposal for a "reflective practicum" suggests a way forward in integrating new found theories and techniques within the advantages of the studio system.

This study is a scholarly, searching piece of work which advances a new view of architectural education as a prototypical design activity with implications for higher education in general.

Department of Architecture, University of Sheffield
United Kingdom
March 1985

Introduction

In the United Kingdom, as in the United States and many other nations throughout the world, there has been in recent years a surge of interest in architectural education. Within the schools of architecture, in the professional associations of educators and practitioners, in new journals devoted to the topic, and even in newly appointed national commissions, there has been a ferment of discussion and debate.

Much of the debate has been framed in the familiar terms of a perceived imbalance of supply and demand. In the United States, for example, there are signs of a rapidly increasing population of practising architects. In the state of Florida, to take one dramatic instance, the number of resident architects has grown over the past twenty years from about 500 to 3,000, or from a ratio of 10 per 100,000 population to a ration of 27 per 100,000[1]. Over the same time period, not only in Florida but in the United States as a whole, there has been a decline in the percentage of buildings designed by architects. Nevertheless, the number of students enrolled in architectural programs has held steady or increased. Some 37,000 students are now enrolled, of which, however, only one in eight graduates with a degree in architecture; and of these, only thirty percent go on to pass their registration board examinations.[2]

Given the signs of an oversupply of practising professionals, and the narrowing funnel through which students move from school to professional practice, it is striking that, at least in many places, enrolment in schools of architecture has tended to hold up so strongly. supply, in this case, seems to be relatively insensitive to fluctuations in demand. In professional, educational and governmental circles, these contradictory trends have been the subject of vigorous debate. How should the schools, and those who fund the schools, be responding?

Some observers advocate a reduction in supply. In the United Kingdom, for example, one well-known school of architecture has been recently closed. Others argue that in the United States and United Kingdom — as has long been the case in other countries, such as Italy — architectural education has come to function as an alternative form of general liberal arts education. Students choose architecture, as they also choose history or classics, when they have no intention of becoming practising architects. Architecture should be seen, in this view, both as a form of professional training and as an alternative form of general higher education. But such a policy has important implications for the structure and content of architectural education. In what directions should the schools of architecture develop if they are to play this dual role?

A second reason for the surge of interest in architectural education is the growing recognition of changes in the nature and context of architectural practice. In the established circles of industrial nations, practitioners have become aware of the extent to which the design and construction of buildings has become a complex sociotechnical process. At least in the large firms that tend to dominate the profession, the practitioner is coming to be seen less as an individual designer in one-to-one relation with his client than as the manager of a technical team. New domains of applied science and technology — energy management, ecology, building diagnostics, along with the more familiar fields of structural engineering, lighting, acoustics, soil mechanics, site planning and landscape architecture — are seen to have central roles in the building process. Computers, still in their infancy as far as designing and building are concerned, are moving toward a leading, though still ill-defined, role. A recent National Academy of Sciences conference on computers in building design, intended for several hundred participants, attracted several thousand. Architects have begun to find themselves in competition with other professions, such as engineers and quantity surveyors, for the roles of design team management. There are changes in the institutional structure of architectural practice, as real estate development, construction, design and building management firms come into new relationships with one another. Some architects have begun to play entrepreneurial roles in the development process. In the non-industrialized nations, and in the lower income segments of industrialized nations, some architects have learned to function, not as designers of buildings but as enablers of self-help design and construction carried out by indigenous populations. There is an emerging field of "community architecture" in which architects seek to function as advocates and providers of technical assistance to community clients. Leading practitioners and educators have long since begun to wonder whether traditional architectural education — especially the sort that as one former student put it, "tends to make us all into little LeCorbusiers" — can equip students for effective participation in these emergent roles.

The task of answering this question has been made more difficult by two very robust features of contemporary architectural education.

In the twentieth century, architectural education, like architectural practice, has been resolutely pluralistic. Architecture tends to have been dominated by the work of "great men", such as Wright, LeCorbusier, Mies, Aalto, Kahn, and by the schools of thought, or better yet, the movements, built up around them. The pronouncements of these great men and their followers, and the debates among them, have tended to adopt a distinctly ideological tone. Moreover, the several voices claiming to present Architecture have tended to stand not only for different images of desirable buildings, appreciative systems and priorities of attention, but for different views of the design process and ways of framing the architect's role. Caught in the cross-fire of architectural movement and competing images and paradigms of practice, the architectural schools have tended to take one of two positions — either to ally themselves with one of the competing voices, adopting its images, style, and views of relevant knowlege or to present a "supermarket" of alternatives, leaving the student (however poorly suited to the task he or she may be) the burden of choice or synthesis.

Underlying these divisions of schools of thought and paradigms of practice, there is a more fundamental division. Historically, architecture has been a hybrid, or bimodal, profession, seen on the one hand as an art, with roots in the monuments of the ancient, medieval, and Renaissance worlds and, on the other hand, as a social function, providing structures and spaces within which the life and work of society are conducted. As "artist", the architect is seen as a giver of forms, constrained — perhaps unhappily — by the demands and the limited resources of his client or patron. As a functional specialist, the architect is seen as bringing his design

3

competence and special knowledge to the fulfilment of individual and social needs. In the world of contemporary architectural practice and education, the two views of the profession tend to polarize, each view suggesting a very different answer to the questions posed by the shifts in architectural practice. If the architect is, indeed, an artist, what business has he with the technical management of design teams? and if he is primarily a functional specialist, what business has he with the traditions of the great architectural artists around whom the prevailing movements have developed?

In a world characterized by this division, and by a babble of contending voices claiming to represent Architecture, it is exceedingly difficult for the profession to speak with ones voice in its efforts to respond to the changing context of practice. It is exceedingly difficult for the schools to decide how the traditional patterns of education should be extended or modified to include the domains of knowledge and competence thought to be essential to emergent architectural roles.

Finally, it is important to note that, in their efforts to grapple with the issues whose complexity has been sketched above, the architectural educators speak from a platform lacking stability and status. In the universities — where in the United States, most, and in the United Kingdom, many schools of architecture are located — architecture's place is at the margins. For reasons I will elaborate shortly, architecture tends to fall outside the prevailing norms of the modern, research-based universities. Compared to departments of economics, physics, engineering, or mathematics, its status tends to be low and its standards of accomplishment tend not to be understood. In some universities, for example, professors of architecture gain tenure on the basis of the quality, not of their design portfolios but of their published papers. In times of retrenchment in higher education, departments of architecture are vulnerable.

All of these reasons for the resurgent interest in architectural education have a prudential or premonitory ring. They stem from awareness of threats to the profession or from a recognition that architectural education must change in order to keep up with changes in the world around it. In this essay, however, I shall propose an additional interest in architectural education — an interest affecting not only the practitioners, teachers, and students of architecture but the schools of other

4

professions, including those professions whose status in the universities is highest.

I shall argue that the schools of other professions have a great deal to learn from the unique institution of architectural education, the studio. In the context of the modern research university, the architectural studio is deviant. It is a throwback to an earlier mode of education and an earlier epistemology of practice, which helps to account for its current marginal status in the university. It is the repository of long-standing traditions for education in the artistry of designing. It is a setting for the acquisition of a competence to perform, and it has something important to say to other professional schools increasingly aware of the dilemmas inherent in their more recent traditions of education as the transfer of professional knowledge.[3]

What Nathan Glazer has called the "major" professions of medicine, law, and business, along with such "minor" professions as social work, education, and town planning, [4] are based on an epistemology of practice embedded in the modern research university where these professions have established their schools. On this view, professional competence consists in the application of systematic professional knowledge — at best, scientific knowledge — to the instrumental problems of practice. The professional schools have, in greater or lesser degree, accepted a normative professional curriculum[5] made up of the relevant basic science, the relevant applied science, and a "practicum" in office, clinic, field-work or laboratory, where students are supposed to apply to everyday practice the scientific knowledge they have acquired in the classroom. But, increasingly, leading practitioners and educators in these professions have become aware of the crucial importance of indeterminate zones of practice which do not lend themselves to the theories and techniques derived from the normative professional curriculum. Their attention has turned to the dilemmas of practice under conditions of complexity, uncertainty, and uniqueness. In the face of increasingly strident criticisms from the lay public, and from within their own professions, they have become attentive to issues of value-conflict and morality. They have begun to shift their attention from technical expertise to artistry and from problem-solving to problem-setting. And, with this shift of attention, they have begun to question the adequacy of the normative professional curriculum as a preparation for a life in the professions.

5

At its best, the architectural studio is an examplar of education for artistry and problem-setting. With distant origins in the apprenticeships of the medieval guilds and more recent origins in the École des Beaux Arts of the late nineteenth and early twentieth centuries, architectural studios are prototypes of individual and collective learning-by-doing under the guidance and criticism of master practitioners. There are many different types of architectural studios with different pedagogies, emphases on architectural form, technologies, allegiances to competing schools of architectural thought. But there are also certain central, more or less constant features of the studio from which other professions can learn.

What students and studio masters do in the studio is in some ways unlike the reality of architectural practice. It tends, for example, to minimize the laborious rendering of technical detail on which many young practitioners spend a great deal of their time. It tends to leave out such important processes as dealing with building code inspectors and with the conflicting preferences of clients and interest groups. Few studios pay attention to breakdowns of equipment or work-stoppages on the site. Nevertheless, the kinds of inquiry undertaken in the studio are at the heart of architectural practice. Given an architectural program (or brief) and the description of a site, the student must first set a design problem and then go on to solve it. Setting the problem means framing the problematic situation presented by site and program in such a way as to create a springboard for design inquiry. The student must impose his preferences onto the situation in the form of choices whose consequences and implications he must subsequently work out — all within an emerging field of constraints.

The architectural studio has developed traditions of learning-by-doing — the tradition of project-based education, which often seems innovative when it is introduced to other professional schools; the more particular traditions of work, review, and criticism; and the less easily nameable traditions that inform the ways in which groups of students learn from and with one another. These have evolved gradually over many years, and contribute to a rich context for learning-by-doing.

In the context of the studio, some instructors have learned to become not only master practitioners but master coaches. They have learned to respond to the imperative, present in the studio as it is often not in practice, to make design assumptions, strategies and values explicit. They have learned to deal with paradoxes and predicaments that arise whenever students try to acquire competences they perceive as radically new. They have become familiar with the various uses of types of projects, strategies of description, and styles of demonstration and criticism.

Among observers of the professions, it has become commonplace that all competent practice involves a kind of design. Indeed, the language of design has entered into the ordinary languages of many professions other than those usually called "design professions". In medicine, practitioners speak of the design of a process of diagnosis and intervention; in law, cases and arguments are "designed". One eminent student of the professions has argued for a science of design as the fundamental knowlege-base underlying all professional education.[6] Architecture is the very prototype of design activity. It is certainly worth considering that other professions, more recently come to awareness of the need for education in the artistry of practice, can learn from the traditions of the architectural studio and from the experience of the studio-masters.

In order for the lessons of the studio to be made accessible to other professions, however, studio masters must be willing to examine what they already know how to do. They must try to make systematic descriptions of their practice and coaching, and the knowledge and appreciations embedded in them, in spite of the factors that work against systematic self-reflection. Like other practitioners, architects tend to value action over reflection. They tend to take for granted what is most exceptional about their own familiar practice. Perhaps more than other practitioners, they tend to mystify their artistry, treating it defensively as an indescribable something that "either one has or has not". In the universities, where architects see themselves accurately as occupants of the lower rungs on the ladder of status, they may be reluctant to image that they have something important to give other fields. And finally, they may find it extraordinarily difficult to give explicit, accurate, and useful accounts of the understandings implicit in gradually learned competences that have become intuitive.

In view of these impediments, I shall try in this essay to illustrate what such a process of reflection might be like. I do not propose to make an exhaustive, or even a representative, description of the architectural studio.[7] I shall concentrate on a few examples of studio practice, hoping to encourage studio

7

masters to undertake their own more systematic reflections and to interest a wider audience of educators in the unique potential of the architectural studio.

I do not believe, however, that the benefits of such an inquiry will flow only from architects to non-architects. As the schools of architecture revise their own curricula in order to take account of the changing nature of architectural practice, and as they try to work out productive marriages of artistry, applied science and technology, they will profit from a more reflective grasp of the understandings and know-how embedded in their own traditions. And, if they pursue the more deliberate use of architecture as a form of general higher education, they will need to articulate more fully the premises of their bid for educational leadership.

The argument of this essay will be divided into six parts: (1) the dilemmas of contemporary professional education, (2) artistry conceived as reflection-in-action, (3) the architectural studio as a vehicle for education in artistry, (4) the paradox and predicament of learning to design, (5) the artistry of the studio master, and (6) what can be learned from the experience of studio.

Part I: Dilemmas of Contemporary Professional Education

The crisis in confidence in professional knowledge

Although our society has become thoroughly dependent on professionals, so much so that the conduct of business, industry, government, education, and everyday life would be unthinkable without them, there are signs of a growing crisis of confidence in the professions. In many well-publicized scandals, professionals have been found willing to use their special positions for private gain. Professionally designed solutions to public problems have had unanticipated consequences, sometimes worse than the problem they were intended to solve. The public has shown an increasing readiness to call for external regulation of professional practice. Laymen have been increasingly disposed to turn to the courts for defense against professional incompetence or venality. The professional's traditional claims to privileged social position and autonomy of practice have come into question as the public has begun to have doubts about professional ethics and expertise.[1] And in recent years, professionals themselves have shown signs of a loss of confidence in professional knowledge.

Not very long ago, in 1963, the editors of *Daedalus* could introduce a special volume on the professions with the sentence, "Everywhere in American life the professions are triumphant."[2] They noted the apparently limitless demand for professional services, the "shortages" of teachers and physicians, the difficulty of coordinating the proliferating technical specializations, the problem of managing the burgeoning mass of technical data. In the further essays which made up the volume, doctors, lawyers, scientists, educators, military men, and politicians articulated variations on the themes of professional triumph, overload, and growth. There were only two discordant voices. The representative of the clergy complained of declining influence and the "problem of relevance"[3], and the city planner commented ruefully on his profession's lagging understanding of the changing ills of urban areas.[4] Yet in less than a decade the discordant notes had become the dominant ones and the themes of professional triumph had virtually disappeared.

9

In 1972, a colloquium on professional education was held at the Massachusetts Institute of Technology. Participants included distinguished representatives of the field of medicine, engineering, architecture, planning, psychiatry, law, divinity, education, and management. These individuals disagreed about many things, but they held one sentiment in common — a profound uneasiness about their own professions. They questioned whether professionals would effectively police themselves. They wondered whether professionals were instruments of individual well-being and social reform or were mainly interested in the preservation of their own status and privilege, caught up in the very problems they might have been expected to solve. They allowed themselves to express doubts about the relevance and remedial power of professional expertise.

It is perhaps not very difficult to account for this dramatic shift, over a single decade, in the tone of professional self-reflection. Between 1963 and 1972 there had been a disturbing sequence of events, painful for professionals and lay public alike. A professionally instrumented war had been disastrous. Social movements for peace and civil rights had begun to see the professions as elitist servants of established interests. The much-proclaimed shortages of scientists, teachers, and physicians seemed to have evaporated. Professionals seemed powerless to relieve the rapidly shifting "crises" of the cities, poverty, environmental pollution, and energy. There were scandals of Medicare and, at the end of the decade, Watergate. Cumulatively, these events created doubts about professionally conceived strategies of diagnosis and cure. They pointed to the overwhelming complexity of the phenomena with which professionals were trying to cope. They led to scepticism about the adequacy of professional knowledge, with its theories and techniques, to cure the deeper causes of societal distress.

Sharing, in greater or lesser degree, these sentiments of doubt and unease, the participants in the MIT colloquium tried to analyse their predicament.

Some of them believed that social change had created problems ill-suited to the traditional division of labor. A noted engineer observed that "education no longer fits the niche, or the niche no longer fits education". The dean of a medical school spoke of the complexity of a huge health care system only marginally susceptible to the interventions of the medical profession. The dean of a school of management referred to the puzzle of educating managers for judgment and action under conditions of uncertainty.

Some were troubled by the existence of an irreducible residue of art in professional practice. The art deemed indispensable even to scientific research and engineering design seemed resistant to codification. As one participant observed, "if it's invariant and known, it can be taught; but it isn't invariant."

Professional education emphasized problem-solving, but the most urgent and intractable issues of professional practice were those of problem-finding. "Our interest", as one participant put it, "is not only how to pour the concrete for the highway, but what highway to build? When it comes to designing a ship, the question we have to ask is, which ship makes sense in terms of the problems of transportation?"

And representatives of architecture, planning, social work, and psychiatry spoke of the pluralism of their schools. Different schools held different and conflicting views of the competences to be acquired, the problem to be solved, even of the nature of the professions themselves. A leading professor of psychiatry described his field as a "babble of voices".

Finally, there was a call for the liberation of the professions from the tyranny of the university-based professional schools. Everett Hughes, one of the founders of the sociology of the professions, declared that "American universities are products of the late 19th and early 20th centuries. The question is, how do you break them up in some way, at least get some group of young people who are free of them? How do you make them free to do something new and different?"

The years that have passed since the 1972 colloquium have tended to reinforce its conclusions. In the early 1980's, no profession could celebrate itself in triumphant tones. In spite of the continuing eagerness of the young to embark on apparently secure and remunerative professional careers, professionals are still criticized, and criticize themselves, for failing both to adapt to a changing social reality and to live up to their own standards of practice. There is widespread recognition of the absence or loss of a stable institutional framework of purpose and knowledge within which professions can live out their roles and confidently exercise their skills.

In retrospect, then, it is not difficult to see why participants in the 1972 colloquium should have puzzled over the troubles of their professions. They were beginning to become aware of the indeterminate zones of practice − the situations of complexity and uncertainty, the unique cases that require artistry, the elusive task of problem-setting, the multiplicity of professional identities — that have since become increasingly visible and problematic. Nevertheless, there is something strange about their disquiet. For professionals in many different fields do sometimes find ways of coping effectively, even wisely, with situations of complexity and uncertainty. If the element of art in professional practice is not invariant, known, and teachable, it does appear occasionally to be learnable. Problem-setting is an activity in which some professionals engage with recognizeable skill. And students and practitioners do occasionally make thoughtful choices from among the multiple views of professional identity.

Why, then, should a group of eminent professionals have been so troubled by the evidence of indeterminacy in professional practice?

It was not, I think, that they were unaware of the ways in which some practitioners cope well with situations of indeterminacy. Indeed, they might easily have counted themselves among that number. Rather, I suspect, they were troubled because they could not readily account for the coping process. Complexity and uncertainty are sometimes dissolved, but not by means of applying specialized knowledge to well-defined tasks. Artistry is not reducible to the exercise of describable routines. Problem-finding has no place in a body of knowledge concerned exclusively with problem-solving. In order to choose among competing paradigms of professional practice, one cannot rely on professional expertise. The eminent professionals were disturbed, I think, to discover that the competences they were beginning to see as central to professional practice had no place in their underlying model of professional knowledge.

The Dominant Model of Professional Knowledge

The epistemology of professional practice which dominates most thinking and writing about the professions, and is built into the very structure of professional schools and research institutions, has been clearly set forth in two recent essays on professional education. Both of these treat rigorous professional practice as an exercise of technical rationality, that is, as an application of research-based knowledge to the solution of problems of instrumental choice.

Edgar Schein, in his *Professional Education*, proposes a threefold division of professional knowledge:

12

(1) An *underlying discipline* or *basic science* component upon which the practice rests or from which it is developed.
(2) An *applied science* or *"engineering"* component from which many of the day-to-day diagnostic procedures and problem-solutions are derived.
(3) A *skills and attitudinal* component that concerns the actual performance of services to the client, using the underlying basic and applied knowledge.[5]

In Schein's view, these components constitute a hierarchy which may be read in terms of application, justification and status. The application of basic science yields engineering, which in turn provides models, rules and techniques applicable to the instrumental choices of everyday practice. The actual performance of services "rests on" applied science, which rests, in turn, on the foundation of basic science. In the epistemological pecking order, basic science is highest in methodological rigor and purity, its practitioners superior in status to those who practice applied science, problem-solving, or service delivery.

Nathan Glazer, in a much-quoted article, argues that the schools of such professions as social work, education, divinity and town planning are caught in a hopeless predicament.[6] These "minor" professions, beguiled by the success of the "major" professions of law, medicine and business, have tried to substitute a basis in scientific knowledge for their traditional reliance on experienced practice. In this spirit, they have placed their schools within universities. Glazer believes, however, that their aspirations are doomed to failure. The "minor" professions lack the essential conditions of the "major" ones. They lack stable institutional contexts of practice, fixed and unambiguous ends with "settle men's minds",[7] and a basis in systematic scientific knowledge. They cannot apply scientific knowledge to the solving of instrumental problems, and they are, therefore, unable to produce a rigorous curriculum of professional education.

Can these fields (education, city planning, social work and divinity) settle on a fixed form of training, a fixed content of professional knowledge, and follow the models of medicine, law and business? I suspect not because the discipline of a fixed and unambiguous end in a fixed institutional setting is not given to them. And *thus* (my emphasis) the base of knowledge which is umambiguously indicated as relevant for professional education is also not given.[8]

Glazer and Schein share an epistemology of professional practice rooted historically in the positivist philosophy which so powerfully shaped both the modern university and the modern conception of the proper relationship of theory and practice.[9] Rigorous professional practice is conceived as essentially technical. Its rigor depends on the use of describable, testable, replicable techniques derived from scientific research, based on knowledge that is objective, consensual, cumulative and convergent. On this view, for example, engineering is an application of engineering science; rigorous management depends on the use of management science; and policy-making can become rigorous when it is based on policy-science.

Practice can be construed as technical, in this sense, only when certain things are kept clearly separate from one another. Deciding must be kept separate from doing. The rigorous practitioner uses his professional knowledge to *decide* on the means best suited to his ends, his *action* serving to "implement" technically sound decisions. Means must be clearly separated from ends. Technical means are variable, appropriate or inappropriate according to the situation. But the ends of practice must be "fixed and unambiguous", like Glazer's examples of profit, health and success in litigation; how is it possible, otherwise, to evolve a base of applicable professional knowledge? And finally, research must be kept separate from practice. For research can yield new knowledge only in the protected setting of the scholar's study or in the carefully controlled environment of a scientific laboratory, whereas the world of practice is notoriously unprotected and uncontrollable.

These tenets of the positivist epistemology of practice are still built into our institutions, even when their inhabitants no longer espouse them. Just as Thorsten Veblen propounded some seventy years ago,[10] the university and the research institute are sheltered from the troublesome world of practice. Research and practice are presumed to be linked by an exchange in which researchers offer theories and techniques applicable to practice problems and practitioners, in return, give researchers new problems to work on and practical tests of the utility of research results. The normative curriculum of professional education, as Schein describes it, still follows the

14

hierarchy of professional knowledge. First, students are exposed to the relevant basic science, then to the relevant applied science, and finally to a practicum in which they are presumed to learn to apply classroom knowledge to the problems of practice. Medical education offers the prototype for such a curriculum, and its language of "diagnosis", "cure", "laboratory", and "clinic" have long since diffused to other professions.

From the perspective of this model of professional knowledge, it is not difficult to understand why practitioners should be puzzled by their own performance in the indeterminate zones of practice. Their performance does not fit the criteria of technical rationality; it cuts across the dichotomies built into the positivist epistemology of practice. Artistry, for example, is not only in the deciding but also in the doing. When planners or managers convert an uncertain situation into a solvable problem, they construct — as John Dewey pointed out long ago — not only the means to be deployed but the ends-in-view to be achieved. In such problem-setting, ends and means are reciprocally determined. And often, in the unstable world of practice, where methods and theories developed in one context are unsuited to another, practitioners function as researchers, inventing the techniques and models appropriate to the situation at hand.

The Dilemma of Rigor or Relevance

For practitioners, educators and students of the professions, the positivist epistemology of practice contributes to an urgent dilemma of rigor or relevance.

Given the dominant view of professional rigor, the view which prevails in the intellectual climate of the universities and is embedded in the institutional arrangements of professional education and research, rigorous practice depends on well-formed problems of instrumental choice to whose solution research-based theory and technique are applicable.[11] But real-world problems do not come well-formed. They tend to present themselves, on the contrary, as messy, indeterminate, problematic situations. When a civil engineer worries about what road to build, for example, he does not have a problem he can solve by an application of locational techniques or decision-theory. He confronts a complex and ill-defined situation in which geographic, financial, economic and political factors are usually mixed up together. If he is to arrive at a well-formed problem, he must construct it from the materials

15

of the problematic situation. And the problem of problem-setting is not a well-formed problem.[12]

When a practitioner sets a problem, he chooses what he will treat as the "things" of the situation. He decides what he will attend to and what he will ignore. He names the objects of his attention and frames them in an appreciative context which sets a direction for action. A vague worry about hunger or malnourishment may be framed, for example, as a problem of selecting an optimal diet. But situations of malnourishment may be framed in many different ways.[13] Economists, environmental scientists, nutrition scientists, agronomists, planners, engineers and political scientists debate over the nature of the malnourishment problem, and their discussions have given rise to a multiplicity of problem-setting worthy of *Rashomon*. Indeed, the practice of malnourishment planning is largely taken up with the task of constructing the problem to be solved.

When practitioners succeed in converting a problematic situation to a well-formed problem, or in resolving a conflict over the proper framing of a practitioner's role in a situation, they engage in a kind of inquiry which cannot be subsumed under a model of technical problem-solving. Rather, it is through the work of naming and framing that the exercise of technical rationality becomes possible.

Similarly, the artistic processes by which practitioners sometimes make sense of unique cases, and the art they sometimes bring to everyday practice, do not meet the prevailing criteria of rigorous practice. Often, when a competent practitioner recognizes in a maze of symptoms the pattern of a disease, constructs a basis for coherent design in the peculiarities of a building site, or discerns an understandable structure in a jumble of materials, he does something for which he cannot give a complete or even a reasonably accurate description. Practitioners make judgments of quality for which they cannot state adequate criteria, display skills for which they cannot describe procedures or rules.

By defining rigor only in terms of technical rationality, we exclude as non-rigorous much of what competent practitioners actually do, including the skilful performance of problem-setting and judgment on which technical problem-solving depends. Indeed, we exclude the most important components of competent practice.

In the varied topography of professional practice, there is a high, hard ground which overlooks a swamp. On the high ground, manageable problems lend themselves to solution through the use of research-based theory and technique. In the swampy lowlands, problems are messy and confusing and incapable of technical solution. The irony of this situation is that the problems of the high ground tend to be relatively unimportant to individuals or to society at large, however great their technical interest may be, while in the swamp lie the problems of greatest human concern. The practitioner is confronted with a choice. Shall he remain on the high ground where he can solve relatively unimportant problems according to his standards of rigor, or shall he descend to the swamp of important problems and non-rigorous inquiry?

Consider medicine, engineering and agronomy, three of Glazer's major or near-major professions. In these fields, there are areas in which problems are clearly defined, goals are relatively fixed, and phenomena lend themselves to the categories of available theory and technique. Here, practitioners can function effectively as technical experts. But when one or more of these conditions is lacking, competent performance is no longer a matter of exclusively technical expertise. Medical technologies like kidney dialysis or tomography have created demands which stretch the nation's willingness to invest in medical care. How should physicians behave? How should they try to influence or accommodate to health policy? Engineering solutions which seem powerful and elegant when judged from a relatively narrow perspective may have a wider range of consequences which degrade the environment, generate unacceptable risk, or put excessive demands on scarce resources. How should engineers take these factors into account in their actual designing? When agronomists recommend efficient methods of soil cultivation that favor the use of large land-holdings, they may undermine the viability of the small family farms on which peasant economies depend. How should the practice of agronomy take such considerations into account? These are not problems, properly speaking, but problematic situations from which problems must be constructed. If practitioners choose not to ignore them, they must approach them through kinds of inquiry which are, according to the dominant model of technical rationality, not rigorous.

The doctrine of technical rationality, promulgated and maintained in the universities and especially in the professional schools, infects the young professional-in-training with a hunger for technique. Many students of urban planning, for example, are impatient with anything other than "hard skills". In schools of management, students often chafe under the discipline of endless case-analysis; they want to learn the techniques and algorithms which are, as they see it, the key to high starting salaries. Yet a professional who really tried to confine his practice to the rigorous application of research-based technique would find not only that he could not work on the most important problems but that he could not practice in the real world at all.

Nearly all professional practitioners experience some version of the dilemma of rigor or relevance, and they may respond to it in several ways. They may choose the swampy lowland, deliberately immersing themselves in confusing but crucially important situations. When asked to describe their methods of inquiry, they speak of experience, trial and error, intuition and muddling through. When teachers, social workers or planners operate in this vein, they tend to be afflicted with a nagging sense of inferiority to those who present themselves as models of technical rigor. When physicians or engineers do so, they may be troubled by the discrepancy between the technical rigor of the "hard" zones of their practice and the apparent sloppiness of the "soft" ones.

Practitioners who opt for the high ground confine themselves to a narrowly technical practice and pay a price for doing so. Operations research, systems analysis, policy analysis, and management science are examples of practices built around the use of formal, analytic models. In the early years of the development of these professions, following World War 2, there was a climate of optimism about the power of formal modelling for the solution of real world problems. In subsequent decades, however, there has been a growing recognition of the limits of these techniques, especially in situations of high complexity and uncertainty.[14] Some practitioners have responded by confining themselves to the limited class of problems — for example, to inventory control. Others have continued to develop formal models for use in problems of high complexity and uncertainty, quite undeterred by the troubles incurred whenever a serious attempt is made to put their models into practice. They may become researchers, pursuing an agenda driven by evolving questions of modelling theory and technique, increasingly divergent from the context of actual practice.

They may try, on the other hand, to cut the situations of practice to fit their models, employing for this purpose one of several procrusean strategies. They may, for example, become selectively inattentive to data that do not fit their theories,[15] as educators preserve their confidence in "competency-testing" by ignoring the kinds of competence that competency-testing fails to detect. Physicians or therapists may use junk categories like "patience resistance" to explain away the cases in which an indicated treatment fails to lead to cure.[16] And social workers may try to make their technical expertise effective by exerting unilateral control over the practice situation, for example, by removing "unworthy" clients from the case rolls.

Those who confine themselves to the limited range of technical problems, or cut the situations of practice to fit available models and techniques, seek a world in which technical rationality works. Even those who choose the swamp tend to pay homage to prevailing models of rigor; and what they know how to do, they have no way of describing as rigorous.

Writers about the professions tend to follow similar paths. Both Glazer and Schein, for example, recognize the indeterminate zones of professional practice. But Glazer relegates them to the "minor" professions, of which he despairs. And Schein locates what he calls "divergent" phenomena of uncertainty, complexity, and uniqueness in concrete practice situations, while at the same time regarding professional knowledge as increasingly "convergent". He thinks convergent knowledge may be applied to divergent practice through the exercise of "divergent skills"[17] — about which, however, he is able to say very little. For if divergent skills were treated in terms of theory or technique, they would belong to convergent professional knowledge; and if they are neither theory nor technique, they cannot be described as "knowledge" at all. Rather, they function as a kind of junk category which serves to protect an underlying model of technical rationality.

Yet the epistemology of practice embedded in our universities and research institutions, ingrained in our habits of thought about professional knowledge, and at the root of the dilemma of rigor or relevance, has lost its hold on the field that nurtured it. Among philosophers of science, no-one wants any

19

longer to be called a positivist.[18] There is a rebirth of interest in the ancient topics of craft, artistry and myth, topics whose fate positivism seemed once to have finally sealed. Positivism and the positivist epistemology of practice now seem to rest on a particular *view* of science, one now largely discredited.

It is timely, then, to reconsider the question of professional knowledge. Perhaps there is an epistemology of practice which takes full account of the competence practitioners sometimes display in situations of uncertainty, complexity and uniqueness. Perhaps there is a way of looking at problem-setting and intuitive artistry which presents these activities as describable and susceptible to a kind of rigor that falls outside the boundaries of technical rationality.

Part II: Reflection-in-Action

Reflection-in Action

When we go about the spontaneous, intuitive performance of the actions of everyday life, we show ourselves to be knowledgeable in a special way. Often, we cannot say what it is that we know. When we try to describe it, we find ourselves at a loss, or we produce descriptions that are obviously inappropriate. Our knowing is ordinarily tacit, implicit in our patterns of action and in our feel for the stuff with which we are dealing. It seems right to say that our knowing is *in* our action. And similarly, the workday life of the professional practitioner reveals, in its recognitions, judgments and skills, a pattern of tacit knowing-in-action.

Once we put aside the mode of technical rationality, which leads us to think of intelligent practice as an *application* of knowledge to instrumental decisions, there is nothing *strange* about the idea that a kind of knowing is inherent in intelligent action. Commonsense admits the category of know-how, and it does not stretch common sense very much to say that the know-how is *in* the action — that a tightrope walker's know-how, for example, lies in, and is revealed by, the way that he takes his trip across the wire, or that a big-league pitcher's know-how is in his way of pitching to a batter's weakness, changing his pace, or distributing his energies over the course of a game. There is nothing in commonsense to make us say that know-how consists in rules or plans which we entertain in the mind prior to action. Although we sometimes think before acting, it is also true that in much of the spontaneous behaviour of skilful practice we reveal a kind of knowing which does not stem from a prior intellectual operation.

As Gilbert Ryle put it:

> What distinguishes sensible from silly operations is not their percentage but their procedure, and this holds no less for intellectual than for practical performances. "Intelligent" cannot be defined in terms of "knowing *that*"; "thinking what I am doing does not connote "both thinking what to do and doing it." When I do

something intelligently . . . I am doing one thing and not two. My performance has a special procedure or manner, not special antecedents.[19]

And Andrew Harrison has recently put the same thought in this pithy phrase: when someone acts intelligently, he "acts his mind".[20]

Examples of these spontaneous, tacit processes of intelligence in action include acts of recognition and judgment, and the exercise of ordinary physical skills.

Michael Polanyi has written about our ability to recognize a face in a crowd.[21] The experience of recognition can be immediate and wholistic. We simply see, all of a sudden, the face of this familiar person. We are aware of no processes of reasoning or calculation — no listing of the particular features peculiar to this person — and we are often unable to describe what we have recognized, that is, what signs distinguish this face from the hundreds of others also present in the crowd.

When the thing we recognize is "something wrong" or "something right", then recognition takes the form of judgment or appreciation. Chris Alexander has called attention to the innumerable judgments of "mismatch" — deviations from a tacit norm — that are involved in the making of a design.[22] And Geoffrey Vickers has gone on to note that not only in artistic judgment but in all of our ordinary judgments of quality, we "can recognize and describe deviations from a norm very much more clearly than we can describe the norm itself.[23] A young friend of mine who teaches tennis observes that his students have to be able to feel when they're hitting the ball right, and they have to like that feeling, as compared to the feeling of hitting it wrong; but they need not, and usually cannot, describe either the feeling of hitting it right or what they do to get that feeling. A skilled physician can sometimes recognize "a case of . . ." the moment a person walks into his office. The act of recognition comes immediately and as a whole; the physician may or may not be able to say, subsequently, just what led to his initial judgment.

Polanyi has described our ordinary tactile appreciation of the surface of materials. If you ask a person what he feels when he explores the surface of a table with his hand, he is apt to say that the table feels rough or smooth, sticky or slippery, but he is unlikely to say that he feels a certain compression and abrasion of his fingertips — though it must be from this kind of feeling that he gets to his appreciation of the table's surface. Polanyi speaks of perceiving *from* these fingertip sensations *to* the qualities of the surface. Similarly, when we use a stick to probe a hidden place, we focus not on the impressions of the stick on our hand but on the qualities of the place which we apprehend through these tacit impressions. To become skilful in the use of a tool is to learn to appreciate, as it were, directly, the qualities of materials that we apprehend *through* the tacit sensations of the tool in our hand.

Chester Barnard has written of "non-logical processes" that we cannot express in words, as a process of reasoning, but only by a judgment, decision, or action.[24] A child who has learned to throw a ball makes immediate judgments of distance which he coordinates, tacitly, with the feeling of bodily movement involved in the act of throwing. A high-school boy, solving quadratic equations, has learned to carry out a sequence of operations spontaneously, though he may not be able to describe the program he follows. A practiced accountant of Barnard's acquaintance could "take a balance sheet of considerable complexity and within minutes or even seconds get a significant set of facts from it", though he could not describe in words the recognitions and calculations that entered into his performance. Similarly, we are able to execute, spontaneously, each complex performance as crawling, walking, riding a bicycle, juggling, without having to think, in any conscious way, what we are doing, without having to describe in words the actions we are carrying out, and often without being able to give a verbal description even approximately faithful to our performance.

Our spontaneous responses to the phenomena of everyday life do not always work. Sometimes our spontaneous knowing-in-action yields unexpected outcomes and we react to the surprise by a kind of thinking what we are doing while we are doing it, a process I call *reflection-in-action*.

Sometimes this sort of process takes the form of ordinary, on-line problem-solving. It may not be associated with a high degree of skill but with the efforts of an amateur to acquire a skill. Recently, for example, I built a wooden gate. The gate was made of wooden pickets and strapping. I had made a drawing of it, and figured out the dimensions I wanted, but I had not reckoned with the problem of keeping the structure square. I noticed, as I began to nail the strapping to the pickets, that the structure wobbled. I knew that when I nailed in a diagonal piece, the structure would become rigid. But how could I be sure that, at the moment I nailed in the diagonal, the structure was square? I stopped to think. There came to mind a vague memory about diagonals — that in a square, the diagonals were equal. I took a yard stick, intending to measure the diagonals; but I found it difficult to make these measurements without moving, and altering the structure. It occurred to me to use a piece of string. Then it became apparent that I need precise locations from which to measure the diagonal from corner to corner. After several frustrating trials, I decided to locate the center point at each of the corners (by crossing diagonals at each corner), hammered in a nail at each of the four center points, and used the nails as anchors for the measurement string. It took several moments to figure out how to adjust the structure so as to correct the errors I found by measuring, and when I had the diagonals equal, I nailed in the piece of strapping that made the structure rigid.

Here — in an example that must have its analogues in the experience of amateur carpenters the world over — my intuitive way of going about the task led me to a surprise (the discovery of the wobble) which I interpreted as a problem. Stopping to think, I invented procedures to solve the problem, discovered further unpleasant surprises, made further corrective inventions, including the several minor inventions necessary to make the idea of string-measurement and diagonals work. Ordinarily, we might call such a process "trial and error", which it certainly is. But we might give a more articulated description of it in terms of the following schema:

To begin with, the starting condition of reflection-in-action is the repertoire of routinized responses that skilful practitioners bring to their practice. This is what I call the practitioner's *knowing-in-action*. It can be seen as consisting of strategies of action, understanding of phenomena, ways of framing the problematic situations encountered in day-to-day experience. It is acquired through training, or through on-the-job experience. It is usually tacit, and it is delivered spontaneously, without conscious deliberation. It works, in the sense of yielding intended consequences, so long as practice situations fall within the boundaries of the normal and routine. It is a dynamic know*ing* process, rather than a static body of know*ledge*, in the sense that it takes the form of continuing detection and correction of error, on-line fine-tuning, all within the framework of a relatively unchanging system of understanding.

A process of continual adjustment in the service of maintaining a sense of constancy. As Gregory Bateson put it, "The more things are the same, the more change (to keep them the same)".

Sometimes, however, there are *surprises*. These take the form of unanticipated events which do not fit existing understandings, fall outside the categories of knowing-in-action. They are anomalous, and *if they are noticed*, they yield uncertainty — meaning not merely that one cannot predict for sure what will happen but that, at least for a time, one cannot make sense of the situation.

Often, such surprises appear as *unique* events — things one has never seen before and may never see again.

Often, they are associated with conflicting values, conflicting ways of framing the problematic situation, even conflicting paradigms of practice. These are tensions or contradictions in what Geoffrey Vickers called the appreciative system of the practitioner.

Together, uncertainty, uniqueness, value-conflict, make up what I call the *indeterminate zones of practice.*

In these zones, competence takes on a new meaning. There is a demand for reflection, though turning to the surprising phenomena and, at the same time, back on itself to the spontaneous knowing-in-action that triggered surprise. It is as though the practitioner asked himself, "What *is* this?" and at the same time, "How have I been *thinking* about this?"

Such reflection must be at least in some degree conscious. It converts tacit knowing-in-action to explicit knowledge for action.

It must take place in the *action-present* — the period of time in which thinking can still make a difference to the outcomes of action.

It has a *critical* function, questioning and challenging the assumptional basis of action, and a *restructuring* function, reshaping strategies, understanding of phenomena, and ways of framing problems.

Thinking gives rise to *experimenting* — but to a particular kind of experimenting, unique to practice, like and unlike the experience of laboratory science. It occurs on-the-spot, in the practice situation. It consists in actions that function in three ways, to *test* new understandings ("What is going on here?"), to *explore* new phenomena ("What else looks odd here?"), and to *affirm or negate the moves* by which the practitioner tries to

25

change things for the better ("How can we get this under control?").

On-the-spot experiment may "work", in the sense that you get what you intend and/or like what you get. Or it may yield further surprises, pleasant or unpleasant. In these instances, we can think of the inquirer moving in the situation and the situation *"talking back"* to the inquirer, triggering a reframing of the problem, a re-understanding of what is going on. The entire process then has the quality of a *reflective "conversation with the situation"*.

These are examples of reflection-in-action drawn from other domains of professional practice:

— A *banker's* judgment of credit risks: Sometimes all the customer's numbers look right but to an experienced banker something still "feels wrong". The banker then experiments on-the-spot to test his intuitive feeling about the situation. (Note that, in such a case, reflection begins with attention to the *feeling*, which is treated as information. The banker asks, "What am I picking up that causes me to feel this?".)

— A *physician* who, recognizing that 85% of the cases that comes into his office are not in the book, responds to unique, anomalous configurations of symptoms by inventing and testing a new diagnosis.

A *market researcher* who is attentive to the market's response to a new product introduction. She listens to what the market is telling her, by its behaviour, about the meaning of the product, sometimes recasting it away from initial production definition toward the unanticipated uses the market has discovered. (As in the case of Scotch Tape.)

— Similarly, *planners* who detect the unanticipated meanings planned interventions have for those affected by them. They may construe these deviations from intentions not as "failure" but as a sign that they have misunderstood the problem they were trying to solve. (As in the case of housing allowances.)

— *Managers* who engage a failure to perform, like a plant that fails to deliver products on time. As the manager explores the situation with his colleagues, he may unearth a normal *Rashomon* of conflicting views of the problem. And he may seek to mobilize his staff in a continuing inquiry which is at once exploratory, aimed at testing understandings of the situation, and aimed at fixing it. Note that, in such a case, the manager's reflection-in-action entails organizational inquiry which may result in a critically important kind of *organizational learning.*

Many such examples of reflection-in-action occur in the indeterminate zones of practice — uncertain, unique or value-conflicted. Depending on the context and the practitioner, such reflection-in-action may take the form of on-the-spot problem-solving, theory-building, or re-appreciation of the situation. When the problem at hand proves resistant to readily accessible solutions, the practitioner may rethink the approach he has been taking and invent new strategies of action. When a practitioner encounters a situation that falls outside his usual range of descriptive categories, he may surface and criticize his initial understanding and proceed to construct a new, situation-specific theory of the phenomenon. (The best theories, Kevin Lynch observed, are those we make in the situation.) When he finds himself stuck, he may decide that he has been working on the wrong problem; he may then evolve a new way of setting the problem, a new frame that he tries to impose on the situation.

The objects of his reflection may lie anywhere in the system of understanding and know-how that he brings spontaneously to his practice. Depending on the centrality of the elements he chooses to surface and rethink, more or less of that system may become vulnerable to change. But, systems of intuitive knowing are dynamically conservative, actively defended, highly resistant to change. They tend not to go quietly to their demise, and reflection-in-action — more especially, reflection on reflection-in-action — often takes on a quality of struggle.

In all such cases, the notion of reflection-in-action goes a long way towards describing what we mean when we speak of a practitioner's *artistry.* It is a capacity to combine reflection and action, on-the-spot, often under stress — to examine understandings and appreciations while the train is running, in the midst of performance. It is artistry, in this sense, that enables some individuals to be competent in situations that do not fit the preconceived categories of technique, theory or rule of thumb, that make up the corpus of "professional knowledge". In the indeterminate zones of practice, some practitioners are sometimes able to make sense of uncertain, confusing situations and to test the sense they make.

Their reflection-in-action is not at war with the instrumental problem-solving that we are used to associating with professional competence. Rather, reflection-in-action on the problematic situation at hand may convert "messes" into the well-formed problems to which research-based techniques can be applied. Competent practice, as we are increasingly coming to see, demands a *marriage* of problem-setting and problem-solving.

Professional artistry, in the form of reflection-in-action, is not a rare event. It is true that many practitioners, locked into a view of themselves as technical experts, find little in the world of practice to occasion reflection. For them, uncertainty is a threat; its admission, a sign of weakness. They have become proficient at techniques of selective inattention, the use of junk categories to dismiss anomalous data, procrustean treatment of troublesome situations, all aimed at preserving the constancy of their knowing-in-action. For others — teachers, managers, engineers or artists — reflection-in-action is the "prose" they speak as they display and develop the ordinary artistry of their professional lives. They are more inclined toward, and adept at, reflection on their intuitive inquiry. Nevertheless, in a world where professionalism is still mainly identified with technical expertise, they may feel profoundly uneasy because they cannot describe what they know how to do, cannot justify it as a legitimate form of professional knowledge, cannot increase its scope or depth or quality, cannot with confidence help others to learn it.

For all of these reasons, the study of professional artistry and its acquisition is of critical importance. We should be turning the puzzle of professional knowledge on its head, not seeking only to build up a science applicable to practice but also to reflect on the reflection-in-action already embedded in competent practice. We should be asking such questions as these:

· How is it that some people learn the kinds and levels of reflection-in-action that are associated with artistry?
· What kinds of competences must they have in order to learn? What must they "know already?"
· If reflection-in-action is sometimes, for some people, learnable, is it also teachable? Can one person help another to learn it? and if the answer is "yes",
· What is it that a good coach knows how to do when he helps a student learn to reflect-in-action? In what does his artistry consist?
· And how should our answers to all of these questions be modified to take account of the special conditions that

28

arise when we consider how professional artistry is, and may be, acquired, in a profession whose curriculum is strongly organized around the teaching of systematic, research-based professional knowledge.

In exploring such questions, we will also be pursuing a new epistemology of practice. Perhaps we will be heeding Everett Hughes's call for ways of breaking up the late 19th century traditions of university and the professional school, at least getting some group of young people who are free of them, making them free to do something new and different.

Part III: The Architectural Studio as a Source of Insight into Education for Reflection-in-Action

If we are to explore how some people learn to reflect-in-action, and how others sometimes help them to do so, we must look not to the normative formal curricula of the professional schools (which are, as we have seen, in the need of instruction on this matter) but to other traditions of education for performance — traditions that deviate from the formal professional norms. We might look to the musical conservatory, where performers, conductors and composers learn their trades; to athletic training, where coaches literally coach athletes to improved performance; to the deviant tradition of instruction by the case method, as it has evolved at a number of institutions, perhaps with particular richness at the Harvard School of Business Administration; to apprenticeships of all kinds, in the crafts, industry, office and clinic. We might even explore the informal underside of some of the professional schools, where we may notice what students sometimes do for one another, or what goes on in the problematic practicum that does not fit the norms of the formal curriculum.

In this essay, however, I propose to explore the traditions of the architectural studio.

For several reasons, architecture may seem a strange example of education for reflection-in-action. To begin with, it is an anomalous profession. It crystallized as a profession before the doctrine of technical rationality had established itself, and therefore carries the seeds of an earlier view of professional competence and knowledge. It is a biomodal profession. On the one hand, it is an art, not only in the sense of craft of design, but also because it uses the forum of building and the experience of passage through the spaces of buildings, as a medium of aesthetic expression. On the other hand, architecture is a utilitarian occupation taken up with the functional design of the buildings and infrastructure upon which our society depends. Architecture lives a biomodal life in the world of art and in the world of functional technical performance.

In the universities, architecture occupies a marginal place. Its bimodality makes the university uneasy. And, more than this, architecture is a throwback to an epistemology older than the one around which the modern university was formed. Architecture experiences conflicting pulls — to join the rest of the university in adopting the model of technical rationality, or to put on the self-protective mystique of a unique art.

Just because of its unique and anomalous status in the modern university, however, architecture exemplifies, in a particularly visible and valuable way, the process of reflection-in-action. Architects are designers; they are makers of representations of things to be built. Moreover — unlike lawyers, physicians, managers or engineers, who might also be seen as makers of things (briefs, diagnoses, mechanisms) but tend not to think of themselves that way — architects tend to be self-recognized makers, and the more talented and craftsmen-like among them tend to regard each new project as a unique case. Even if they are tempted to do so (as some are), architects cannot see their profession as mainly concerned with the application of relevant scientific theory and technique. Although there are ancillary sciences useful to specialized aspects of design — soil mechanics, climatology, structural engineering — there exists no usable science of design. Unlike other professions, in which, under the influence of the normative epistemology of practice, artistry is liable to be confused with applied science, architecture is liable to no such confusion. Artistry in design is clearly essential to architectural competence. Hence, in order to make sense of what designers actually do, we need a view of inquiry based on the process of reflection-in-action. It is in architectural designing that we can get direct access to what I shall call "the maker's reflective conversation with his materials" and we can get it, as we cannot in the fine arts, in the service of functional as well as artistic purposes. In architecture, as I shall try to show, we can get clear and vivid access to a process of inquiry prototypical of the process by which practitioners of other professions sometimes cope creatively and rigorously with the unique, uncertain or conflicted situations of their practice.

Moreover, in the architectural studio we have a very old tradition of education for the exercise of artistry. The studio tradition builds examples of practice and critical reflection on practice, into the core experience of learning architectural design. Design education is organized around manageable projects of design, individual or collective, which are more or less closely patterned on projects drawn from actual practice. The studio contains its own traditional events — master demonstrations, "design reviews", "desk crits", "juries" — all of which have grown up around the central theme of practice in designing.

When we gain access to a window on the architectural studio, we have a chance to observe, in a peculiarly accessible form, the process of architectural designing; here, more than in any other context, architects need to make clear to one another what it is they do when they design. And at the same time, we gain access to a traditional institutionalized answer to the question, "What does it mean to learn to reflect-in-action?"

An Example of a Design Review

I ask you to imagine an architectural studio. The setting is a loft-like space in which each of twenty students has arranged his or her own drawing tables, paper, books, pictures and models. This is the space in which students spend much of their working lives, at times talking together, but mostly engaged in private, parallel pursuit of the common design task.

At the beginning of the semester, Quist, the studio master,[1] gave all of the students a "program" — a set of design requirements, in this case, for the design for an elementary school, and a graphic description of the site on which the school is to be built.

In the course of the semester, each student is to develop his own versions of the design, recording his results in preliminary sketches, working drawing and models. At the end of the semester, there will be a "crit" at which the students present their designs to Quist and to a group of outside critics (the "jury"). At intervals throughout the semester, Quist holds design reviews with each student, and it is just such a review that Quist now conducts with one of his students, a first-year student named Petra.

For several weeks Petra has worked on the early phases of her design. She has prepared some drawings. Quist examines these while Petra describes how she is "stuck".

After a while, Quist places a sheet of tracing paper over her sketches and begins to draw over her drawing. As he draws, he talks. He says, for example:

> The kindergarten might go over here . . . then you might
> carry the gallery level through . . . and look down into here.

But as Quist says these things he also draws, placing the kindergarten "here" in the drawing, making the line that "carries the gallery level through". His words do not describe what is already there on paper, but parallel the process by which he makes what is there. Drawing and talking are parallel ways of designing, and together make up what I call the language of designing.

The language of designing is a language of doing architecture, a language game which Quist models for Petra, displaying for her competences he would like her to acquire. but Quist's discourse is also punctuated by parentheses in which he talks *about* designing. He says, for example:

You should begin with a discipline, even if it is arbitrary . . .
and again, the principle is that you work simultaneously
from the unit and from the total and then go in cycles.

These are examples of a language about designing, a metalanguage by means of which Quist describes some features of the process he is demonstrating and by which he introduces Petra, however cursorily, to reflection on the action of designing.

In the protocol which follows, both kinds of language are intertwined.

The protocol. This design review lasts for about twenty minutes, and may be divided into several phases. In the first of these, Petra presents her preliminary sketches and describes the problems she has encountered. He reframes it in his own terms and proceeds to demonstrate the working out of a design solution. There follows a brief interval of reflection on the demonstration to date. Quist then sets out the next steps Petra will have to undertake, including one (the calibration of the grid) which leads him to try to get her to look differently at the representation of the slopes. There is, finally, a coda of reflection on all that has gone before.

Petra's presentation. Petra: I am having trouble getting past the diagrammatic phase — I've written down the problems on this list.

I've tried to butt the shape of the building into contours of the land there — but the shape doesn't fit into the slope. (She has a model with a slightly exaggerated slope; they discuss this.)

I chose the site because it would relate to the field there but the approach is here. So I decided the gym must be here — so (showing rough layout) I have the layout like this.

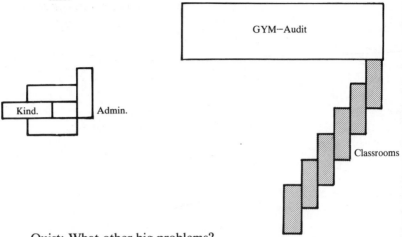

Quist: What other big problems?
Petra: I had six of these classroom units, but they were too small in scale to do much with. So I changed them to this more significant layout (the L-shapes). It relates to one or two, three to four, and five to six grades which is more what I wanted to do educationally anyway. What I have here is a space in which is more of a home base. I'll have an outside/inside which can be used on an outside/inside which can be used — then that opens into your resource library/language thing.

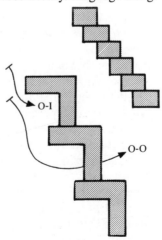

Q: This is to scale?

P: Yes.

Q: Okay, say we have introduced scale. But in the new setup, what about north-south?

(He draws his orientation diagram.)

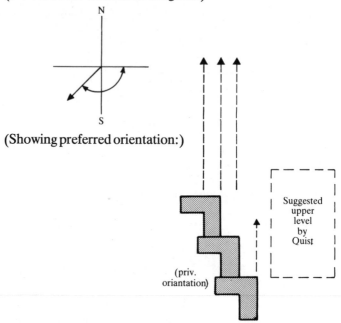

(Showing preferred orientation:)

(priv. oriantation)

P: This is the road coming in here, and I figured the turning circle would be somewhat here —

Petra has taken the contours of the land seriously, accepting the norm that building shape and land contours must fit one another. In her sketches she has tried the experiment of "butting" the shape of her building into the contours of the slope, but the experiment failed; hence the problem.

Petra has also experimented with the size and arrangement of her classroom units. She has found that classrooms must reach a threshold of scale in order to be "significant" enough for design. By regrouping the six smaller classrooms units into three large L-shaped ones, she has tried for "more significant scale". But in doing so, she has also put next to one another the spaces which contain the people who ought most to encounter one another, and she has created a "home base", which sounds like a good place to be, a private outer space which can be used by the kids, and an inner space which has to do, perhaps, with the circulation of the school.

Quists's reframing of the problem. Q: Now this would allow you one private orientation from here and it would generate geometry in this direction. It would be a parallel . . .

P: Yes, I'd thought of twenty feet . . .

Q: You should begin with a discipline, even if it is arbitrary, because the site is so screwy — you can always break it open later.

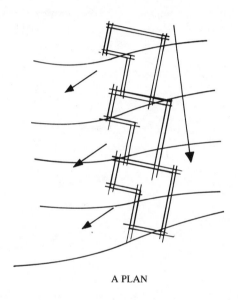

A PLAN

The main problem, in Quist's view, is not of fitting the shape of the buiding to the slope; the site is too "screwy" for that. Instead, coherence must be given to the site in the form of a geometry — a "discipline" — which can be imposed upon it. In the remainder of this phase of the protocol, Quist plays out the consequences of such a move.

Quist's demonstration will now center on the new problem of coordinating the constructed geometry with the "screwy" contours of the slope. But the geometry can be "broken open" again. I think this means that you can dissolve the original discipline in order to try another one, and that you can later make knowing violations of the initial geometry. In Quist's metaphor, the geometry is a sort of armor which can be broken

36

in places, once it has been constructed by consciously departing from it.

Quist's demonstration. Q: Now in this direction, that being the gully and that the hill, that could then be the bridge, which might generate an upper level which could drop down two ways.

(One way from the classroom). We get a total differential potential here from one end of the classroom to far end of the other. There is 15 feet max, right? — so we have as much as 5-foot intervals, which for a kid is maximum height, right? The section through here could be one of nooks in here and the differentiation between this unit and this would be at two levels.

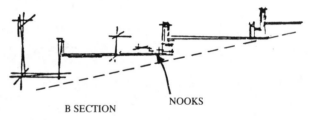

B SECTION   NOOKS

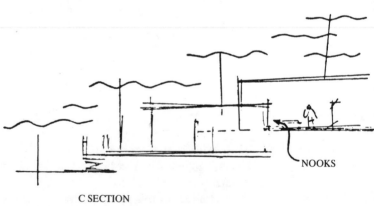

C SECTION

The sketches in Figure 3.1 will help to make clear what is going on in this passage. Quist now proceeds to play out the imposition of the two-dimensional geometry of the L-shaped classroom upon the "screwy" three-dimensional contours of the slope. The L-shaped classrooms are carved into the slope, as in sketch A. The "differential potential", as shown in the sectional sketch B, is from the near end of the classroom lying highest on the slope to the far end of the classroom which is lowest on the slope. The "15 feet max" is given by the total drop in the slope over the distance represented by the three classrooms. The slope is now divided into three levels, one for each of the classrooms, as in B. C shows the "interval" from the ground on one level to the roof of the classroom which stands on the next lower level. The roofs of the classroom will rise five feet above the ground at the next level up, and since five feet is "maximum height for a kid", kids will be able to be in "nooks", as in sketch C, which are approximately as high as the tallest kid.

A drawing experiment has been conducted, and its outcome partially confirms Quist's way of setting the L-shaped classrooms upon the incoherent slope. Classrooms now flow down the slope in three stages, creating protected spaces "maximum height for a kid" at each level. These Quist sees as "nooks", something he could not have done had the level difference come to very much less or more than five feet. To say that the section "could be one of nooks" is to invest these spaces with a special value made possible by the level differences, and it is this which partially confirms Quist's earlier move.

Q: Now you would give preference to that as a precinct which opens out into here and into here and then, of course, we'd have a wall — on the inside there could be a wall or steps to relate in downward. Well, that either happens here or here, and you'll have to investigate which way it should or can go. If it happens this way, the gallery is northwards — but I think the gallery might be a kind of garden — a sort of soft back area to these.

The kindergarten might go over here — which might indicate that the administration over here — just sort of like what you have here — then this works slightly with contours

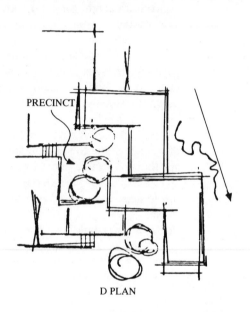

D PLAN

The "nooks" open out into "precincts" whose treatment is a new problem. Retaining walls are required at each level, as in D, but they also mark the different levels. Walls or steps now function as punctuation, marking boundaries and relationships. Quist invites Petra to consider the gallery as a "soft back area", as in sketch D, which would go well with the "hard" classrooms. It can also be "a kind of garden".

The resulting array — L-shaped classrooms, gallery, kindergarten and administration — now "works slightly" with the contours of the slope. With this, Quist harks back to his reframing of Petra's original problem. When she couldn't butt the shape of the building into the screwy slope, Quist imposed on it a geometry of parallels suggested by the L-shaped classrooms. Now the resulting configuration "works slightly" with them. The fit is not very strong, but it is enough.

Q: Then you might carry the gallery level through — and look down into here — which is nice.

Let the land generate some sub-ideas here, which could be very nice. Maybe the cafeteria needn't be such a formal function — maybe it could come into here to get summer sun here and winter here.

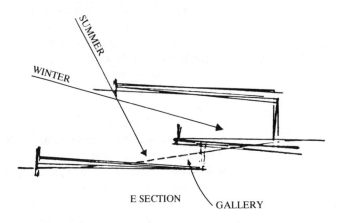

P: Now this gallery is more a general pass-through that anyone can use.
Q: It's a general pass-through that anyone has the liberty to pass through, but it is not a corridor. It marks a level difference from here to here — it might have steps or ramp up to it.
P: My concern is that the circulation through this way — the gallery is generating something awfully cute, but how to pass through here (the library space).
(More examples of Quist answering before they are asked.)
Q: So don't you think of the auditorium as a hard-edged block there.
Quist draws the extension of the gallery as he voices its possibility, imagining the experience of a person who would be following such a path, and he finds the result "nice", once more creating a confirmation of the string of moves he made to date.

Petra has not "let" the cafeteria diverge from its regular geometric shape. He invites her to "soften it" by taking advantage of the site's north-south orientation which will cause the sun to fall on the slope at different angles in summer and winter, as in sketch E. Similarly, he invites her to "soften" the auditorium by relating it to nearby spaces.

Intermediate reflection. P: Where I was hung up was with the original shape; this here makes much more sense.

Q: Much more sense — so that what you have in gross terms is this (he points to his gallery). It is an artifice — the sort of thing Aalto would invent just to give it some order. He's done that on occasion. So in a very minor way, that is the major thing. This repetitive thing is an organized way — there is this which is not repetitive. It is very nice and just the right scale. It also has a sort of verbal order that you can explain to someone.

The gallery, which had begun in Petra's mind as a minor element of the design, a "general pass-through" has now become "in a minor way — the major thing". Quist's reframing and reworking of the problem have led to a reappreciation of the situation, which he now evaluates in terms of norms drawn from several domains — form, scale, and verbal explainability.

Next steps. Q: Now you have to think about size of this middle area. You should have the administration over here.

P: Well, that does sort of solve the problems I had with the administration blocking access to the gym.

Q: No good, horrible — it just ruins the whole idea — but if you move it over there, it is in a better location and opens up the space.

The size of the middle area (not its detailed design) can come up now that they have solved the big problem of adapting the geometry of the classrooms to the screwy slope. In the middle area, they are again concerned with the location of major programmatic elements in relation to one another. And with his criticism of the position of the administration, Quist implies that everything has so far done — the construction of a basic geometry, the imposition of that geometry upon the slope, the creation of the gallery — constitutes an internally coherent whole, all moves having been made with fidelity to the implications set up by earlier moves.

Q: Now the calibration of this becomes important. You just have to draw and draw and try out the different grids.

P: Well, there seemed to be a strange correlation between the two.

Q: No — look at it sideways. It looks much steeper in sections. You see, sections always seem much steeper in reality. Try

41

dividing up a ten degree road — you think you would never make it (draws his slope diagram)

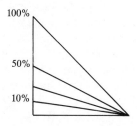

Coda. P: Yes, this was the main thing to get down — how that basic unit — I was thinking in much closer terms coming through the thing.

Q: (Cuts her off) Yeah, and the other thing is the subjection to a common set of geometry. You'll see that that will be a common problem which will come up with everyone, either too much constraint or not enough. How to do that, that is the problem of this problem.

P: It's amazing — intuitively you look at the shape and you know it's wrong, but it's very hard to get down to the reason
. . .

Q: Yeah, well, that is what you are here for. So — I'd worry about the basic geometry of the site. I wouln't concentrate on the roof.

The principle is that you work simultaneously from the unit and from the total and then go in cycles — back and forth, back and forth — which is what you've done a couple of times stutteringly. You have some ideas of the whole which is the grid thing, but you don't know its dimensions. You've done something about this by eliminating that idea, which I think is a good decision. You keep going on — you are going to make it.

Quist returns to his earlier theme ("you should begin with a discipline, even if it is arbitrary"), but now develops it. The basic geometry should bind the designer, but under a norm of moderation. And in fact Quist has continually urged Petra to "soften" her "hard" geometric forms and to depart on occasion from the basic geometry — but only after it has been established.

Quist has been able to give Petra reasons for her intuitions. Now he makes a basic design principle explicit: attention must oscillate between the "whole" and the "unit", the global and

42

the local. Under the metaphor of designing as speaking, Quist contrasts her "stuttering" with his own smooth delivery.

Analysis of the Protocol

Quist's designing takes the form of a reflective conversation with the situation.

At the beginning of the review, Petra is stuck:

I've tried to butt the shape of the building into the contours of the land there — but the shape doesn't fit into the slope.

Quist criticizes her framing of the problem, pointing out that she has tried to fit the shapes of the buidings into the contours of a "screwy" slope which offers no basis for coherence. Instead, he resets her problem:"

You should begin with a discipline, even if it is arbitrary . . . you can always break it open later.

Petra should make the screwy site coherent by imposing on it a discipline of her own, a "what if" to be adopted in order to discover its consequences. If these are unsatisfactory, she can always "break it open later".

From "you should begin with a discipline" to "this works slightly with contours", Quist plays out the consequences of the new discipline by carving the geometry into the slope. In the medium of sketch and spatial-action language, he represents buildings on the site through moves which are also experiments. Each move has consequences described and evaluated in terms drawn from one or more design domains. Each has implications binding on later moves. And each creates new problems to be described and solved. Quist designs by spinning out a web of moves, consequences, implications, appreciations and further moves.

Once the smaller classroom units have been made into L-shaped aggregates, they are "more satisfactory in scale", "put grade one next to grade two", and imply ("generate") a "geometry of parallels in this direction". Given these changes, Quist invents a new move: "that being the gully and that the hill, that could then be the bridge". The bridge also generates something new, an upper level which "could drop down two ways".

Each move is a local experiment which contributes to the global experiment of reframing the problem. Some moves are resisted (the shapes cannot be made to fit the contours), while others generate new phenomena. As Quist reflects on the unexpected consequences and implications of his moves, he listens to the situation's back talk, forming new appreciations which guide his further moves. Most significantly, he becomes aware that the gallery he has created, the "soft back area" to the L-shaped classrooms, has become "in a minor way . . . the major thing". Seizing on the gallery's potential, he "extends it here so as to look down into here". Later he carefully avoids placing the administration building on the site in a way that would spoil "the whole idea".

Thus the global experiment in reframing the problem is also a reflective conversation with the situation in which Quist comes to appreciate and then to develop the implications of a new whole idea. The reframing of the problem is justified by the discovery that the new geometry "works slightly with the contours", yields pleasant nooks, views, and soft back areas, and evokes in the situation the potential for a new coherence. Out of reframing of Petra's problem, Quist derives a problem he can solve and a coherent organization of materials from which he can make something that he likes.

Three dimensions of this process are particularly noteworthy: the domains of language in which the designer describes and appreciates the consequences of his moves, the implications he discovers and follows, and his changing stance toward the situation with which he converses.

Design domains. Quist makes his moves in a language of designing which combines drawing and speaking. In this language, words have different roles. When Quist speaks of a cafeteria that could "come down into here to get summer sun here", "an upper level (which could) drop down two ways", "steps to relate in downward", he uses spatial action language. He attributes actions to elements of the design as though they were creating form and organizing space. At the same time, he anticipates the experienced felt-path[4] of a user of the building who could find that the upper level drops down or that the steps relate in downwards. Quist also uses words to name elements of design ("steps", a "wall", an "administration"), to describe the consequences and implications of moves and to reappreciate the situation.

Elements of the language of designing can be grouped into clusters, of which I have identified twelve (figure 3.2). These design domains contain the names of elements, features, relations, and actions, and of norms used to evaluate problems, consequences and implications. As he designs, quist draws on a repertoire of design domains to fulfill a variety of constructive, descriptive and normative functions.

FIGURE 3.2
Normative Design Domains

Domains	Definitions	Examples
Program/Use	Functions of buildings or building components; uses of building or site; specification for use	"gym", "auditorium", "classroom"; "5″, which is maximum height for a kid"; "no city will plow a road that steep"
Siting	Features elements, relations of the building site	"land contour", "slope", "hill", "gully"
Building Elements	Building or components of buildings	"gym", "kindergarten", "ramp", "wall", "roof", "steps"
Organization of Space	Kinds of spaces and relations of spaces to one another	"a general pass-through", "outside/outside", "layout"
Form	(1) Shape of building or component (2) Geometry (3) Markings of organisation of space (4) Experienced felt-path of movement through spaces	"hard-edged block", "a geometry of parallels", "marks a level difference from here to here", "carry the gallery through and look down into here, which is nice"
Structure/Technology	Structures, technologies, and processes used in building	"a construction module for these classrooms"
Scale	Magnitudes of building and elements in relation to one another	"a 20′ parallel", "too small in scale to do much with", "just the right scale"
Cost	Dollar cost of construction	(none in this protocol)
Building Character	Kind of building, as sign of style or mode of building	("warehouse", "hangar", "beach cottage" — but not in this protocol)
Precedent	Reference to other kinds of buildings, styles or architectural modes	"an artifice . . . the sort of thing Aalto would invent"
Representation	Languages and notations by which elements of other domains are represented	"look at it in section", "$\frac{1}{16}$ scale model"
Explanation	Context of interaction between designer and others	"the sort of verbal order you could explain to someone"

In the domain of program/use, for example, such terms as "classroom", "administration", and "kindergarten" name buildings according to their uses. Phrases like "maximum height for a kid" and "how to pass through . . . the library space" describe the experience of using the buildings.

In the siting domain, Petra uses "contours of the land" to describe her problem, and Quist uses "hill", "gully" and "slope" to construct some of the early steps by which he carves the geometry into the slope.

In the domain of organization of space, Petra speaks of the "outside/outside" created by her L-shaped classrooms, and Quist characterizes the gallery as "a general pass-through that anyone has the liberty to pass through, but . . . not a corridor".

The domain of form has four meanings, distinct but interrelated. First there are the geometrical shapes of buildings, like Petra's "hard-edged block". There is also the sense of global geometry, as in "the geometry of parallels generated by L-shaped classrooms". There is form as a visible sign of the organization of space, as in Quist's observation that the gallery marks level differences in the slope. And finally, there are frequent references to the felt-paths of those who will travel through the organized space, apprehending the figures, qualities, and relations which arise in the experience of movement from place to place.

In their appreciations of the situation they are shaping, Quist and Petra employ feelingful or associative terms such as "home base", "nook", "garden" and "soft back area". "A kind of garden" is not literally a garden, and the "soft back area" is not literally soft, but the metaphors of "garden" and "soft" are used to convey particular values of experience.

Often moves are found to have consequences and implications that cut across design domains. The retaining walls are necessary to the structural soundness of the buildings carved into the slope, but they also mark off formal differences in the levels of the slope. The gallery, which Petra finds "awfully cute", also creates problems of circulation. When design terms are ambiguous in this way, they may create confusion, but they also call attention to multiple consequences. Terms like "stair", "ramp" and "wall" refer both to particular building elements and to formal functions such as "marking" and "relating in". "Gallery" refers both to an organization of space and to a particular precedent ("the sort of thing Aalto would invent"). Aspiring members of the linguistic community of design learn to detect multiple reference, distinguish particular meanings in context, and use multiple references as an aid to vision across design domains.

The designer's repertoire of domains has a structure of priorities for attending to features of situations. In our protocol, there are many references to organization of space, especially to the location of major building elements such as the gym, turning circle, bridge and kindergarten. There are several references to scale, building elements, program/use, and the several sense of form. But there are only single references in each of the domains of precedent, structure/technology, and explanation. The domains of cost and building character do not appear in the protocol at all. The relative frequency of reference to design domains reveals Quist's priorities for attention at this early stage of process.

Implications. When Petra says,

> This is the road coming in here, and I figured the turning circle would be somewhere here . . .

and when Quist later remarks that

> the kindergarten might go over here — which might indicate that the administration (goes) over here

they are noting the implications of earlier moves for later ones, on the basis of a system of norms that governs the relative placement of major building elements. This system includes norms for access (the administration building's central accessibility to all other units), circulation (ease and clarity of movement from one unit to another), and use ("opening up the space"). Thus a decision to locate a road or a kindergarten "here" has implications for the location of a turning circle or an administration "there". In this sense, there is a literal logic of design, a pattern of "if . . . then" propositions that relates the cumulative sequence of prior moves to the choices now confronting the designer.

Because of the contextual relatedness of norms drawn from the domains of site, program, geometry, felt-path, structure and the like, the designer's moves yield systems of implications. These constitute a discipline. If Petra chooses to "locate the site here because it would relate to the field there . . . (and) the approach is here", then "the gym must be here". As Quist says, however, a discipline can always be broken open later. The implications of prior moves must generally be honored but may be violated in a knowledgable way.

47

The web of moves has many branchings, which complicates the problem by discovering and honoring implications. Given the layering of the classrooms on the slope, for example, there could be "a wall or steps to relate in downwards" which might "happen here or here". There are choice-points. As he refelects-in-action on the situation created by his earlier moves, the designer must consider not only the present choice but the tree of further choices to which it leads, each of which has different meanings in relation to the systems of implications set up by earlier moves. Quist's virtuosity lies in his ability to string out design webs of great complexity. But even he cannot hold in mind an indefinitely expanding web. At some point, he must move from a "what if?" to a decision which then becomes a design node with binding implications for further moves. Thus there is a continually evolving system of implications within which the designer reflects-in-action.

The testing of local moves is partly linked to, and partly independent of, this system of implications. Quist discovers that the three classroom levels carved into the slope yield a "total differentiation potential of fifteen feet maximum" which would permit "as much as five-foot intervals" and he subsequently notices that these spaces, seen in section, could be made into "nooks". Here he affirms a local move because he finds that it has produced a situation out of which he can make something that he likes. In this he makes use of his knowledge of the relations between slopes of various grades and their uses. But he finds further support for the dimensions of the geometry he has carved into the slope when he discovers that the resulting configuration "works slightly with contours". His method of carving the geometry of the classrooms into the slope is affirmed in one way when he sees it as a local experiment and in another way when he sees it as part of a global experiment.

Moves also lead to the apprehension of new problems such as the treatment of the "precincts" which flow out from the nooks, and they lead to new potentials for the creation of desirable artefacts such as the softening of the hard-edged shape of the cafeteria by allowing it to "come down into here to get summer sun here and winter sun here". In the designer's conversation with the materials of his design, he can never make a move which has only the effects intended for it. His materials are continually talking back to him, causing him to apprehend unanticipated problems and potentials. As he

48

appreciates such new and unexpected phenomena, he also evaluates the moves that have created them.

Thus the designer evaluates his moves in a threefold way: in terms of the desirability of their consequences judged in categories drawn from the normative design domains, in terms of their conformity to or violation of implications set up by earlier moves, and in terms of his appreciation of the new problems or potentials they have created.

Shifts in stance. As Quist spins out his web of moves, his stance toward the design situation undergoes a series of changes.

Sometimes he speaks of what "can" or "might" happen, and sometimes of what "should" or "must" happen. He shifts from a recognition of possibility and freedom of choice to an acceptance of the imperatives which follow from choice. He urges Petra to step into the problem freely, imposing her own constructs upon it. Without this freedom, there can be no "what if?" But he also calls attention to the discipline of implications generated by her moves. The geometry of the L-shaped classrooms must be followed. Degrees of slope imply constraints on possible uses of the site. Implications for access to sun, circulation, boundary markings, nook-ness, street plowing, consistency of scale, access to gym or administration, fate of trees are at stake in a relatively uncomplicated series of moves. As Quist draws out these implications, he demonstrates fidelity to the "musts" by which the freely chosen "what ifs?" are to be judged.

He also demonstrates how the whole is at stake in every partial move. Once a whole idea has been created, a bad placement of the administration can ruin it. Hence the designer must oscillate between the unit and the total, and — as Quist points out in one of his infrequent meta-comments — he must oscillate between involvement and detachment. Quist becomes at times so involved in the local development of forms that the design appears to be making itself. But he also steps back from the projected experience of passage through the space in order to take note of the larger relationships on which the qualities of the whole idea will depend.

Finally, as he cycles through itineration of moves and appreciations of the outcomes of moves, Quist shifts from tentative adoption of a strategy to eventual commitment. This shift enables him to achieve economy of design, simplifying the evolving web of moves to make his thought-experiment manageable.

The Underlying Process of Reflection-in-Action

Petra's problem solving has led her to a dead end. Quist reflects critically on the main problem she has set, reframes it, and proceeds to work out the consequences of the new geometry he has imposed on the screwy site. The ensuing inquiry is global experiment, a reflection-in-action on the restructured problem. Quist spins out a web of moves, subjecting each cluster of moves to multiple evaluations drawn from his repertoire of design domains. As he does so, he shifts from embracing freedom of choice to acceptance of implications, from involvement in the local units to a distanced consideration of the resulting whole, and from a stance of tentative exploration to one of commitment. He discovers in the situation's back-talk a whole new idea which generates a system of implications for further moves. His global experiment is also a reflective conversation with the situation.

It is not difficult to see how a design process of this form might underlie differences of language and style associated with the various schools of architecture. Designers might differ, for example, with respect to the priorities they assign to design domains at various stages of the process. They might focus less on the global geometry of buildings, as Quist does, than on the site or on the properties and potentials of materials. They might let the design depend more heavily on the formal implications of construction modules. Their governing images might be framed in terms of building character, and they might allow particular precedents to influence more frankly the order they impose on the site. But whatever their differences of languages, priorities, images, styles, and precedents, they are likely to find themselves, like Quist, in a situation of complexity and uncertainty which demands the imposition of an order. From whatever sources they draw such an initial discipline, they will treat its imposition on the site as a global experiment whose results will be only dimly apparent in the early stages of the process. They will need to discover its consequences and implications. And though they may differ from Quist in their way of appreciating these, they will, like him, engage in a conversation with the situation they are shaping. Although their repertoire of meaning may be different from Quist's, they are likely to find new and unexpected meanings in the changes they produce and to redirect their moves in response to such discoveries. And if they are good designers, they will reflect-in-action on the situation's talk-back, shifting stance as they do so from "what if?" to recognition of implications, from involvement in the unit to consideration of the total, and from exploration to commitment.

Some General Themes of Reflection-in-Action

Quist has reflected critically on Petra's framing of the problem. He has conducted an on-the-spot drawing experiment in reframing the problem. And, in the process, he has conducted a reflective conversation with the materials of the design situation.

Quist has not applied to the particular situation before him the general rules drawn from his past experience. On the other hand, it is clear that he does not make use of his earlier experience of screwy sites. His experience is available to him, I think, in the form of a repertoire of particular situations, exemplars and images, in terms of which he is able to see the new situation. He constructs variations on themes with which he is familiar. Seeing the new situation as an element, or elements, of his repertoire, and doing in the new situation as he has done before, he is able to make use of his past experience without reducing the new situation to features that conform to a set of familiar rules.

He carried out a process of on-the-spot experimentation that is partly like and partly unlike a laboratory experiment. His moves function, at one and the same time, in several different modes of experimentation. He tests a reframing of the problem, he seeks to confirm or disconfirm the hypothesis that the new geometry can be made to work with the contours of the slope, he seeks to affirm his moves by discovering that he can make of their results something that he likes (nooks), and he conducts an exploratory probe of the situation that reveals a new and critically important phenomenon. His experimentation is, in its way, appropriately rigorous.

Part of its rigor is due to the fact that Quist conducts his experiment in the virtual world of the tracing paper. In this virtual world, he is able to carry out the drawing experiments that lead to his discoveries. (If he had to experiment by shovelling dirt on the site, the process would be impossibly long and expensive!) He knows very well how to manipulate his virtual world. Drawing over Petra's drawing, he makes a virtual configuration of buildings on the site that he can see and experience as though real. Of course, his virtual world has its limits. It does not capture wind velocities, snow loads, or work stoppages. But it captures a great deal, and it enables the designer to go back and try something again, to look a second time at what he has done before, to slow down or speed up the pace of experimentation, and to experiment at minimum risk.

It is also worth noting that Quist's is a virtuoso performance. He has learned to string out long and complex webs of moves, consequences, implications and further moves. He is a very fluent speaker of the language of designing and a facile manipulator of his virtual world. He has adopted a stance toward his activity that permits him to commit himself to a course of action and, at the same time, to exhibit what Lisa Peattie has called "double vision". In the back of his mind, even as he pursues his committed strategy, he reserves the right to see and do things differently.

The process of reflection-in-action — and especially, the particular version of it that I call reflective conversation with the materials of the situation — is an essential part of the artistry with which some practitioners sometimes cope with uncertainty, uniqueness, and value-conflict in all domains of professional practice. But architecture, with its special tradition of practice and education, is one of the few occupations in which the process is manifest, honored, and maintained. Even here, I think, the process is still largely implicit. Architects appear to reflect very little on their own practice of reflection-in-action.

Part IV: The Paradox and Predicament of Learning to Design

So far, we have considered the dialogue of Quist and Petra for what it reveals about the design process. Suppose we were to look at it as an example of design *education?* What, then, would we notice? First of all, perhaps, that Petra has been involved in doing something on her own, and that she has gotten stuck. She seems to be unclear, in certain respects, just what it is she should be doing, or has some ideas about it incongruent with Quist's. Quist listens to her "big problems" and then takes over, providing a master demonstration of a process similar to the one Petra is supposed to be carrying out. From time to time, he punctuates his demonstration with reflections on the work he is doing, but even when he is not reflecting *on* designing, he uses the drawing/talking language of designing to make his process accessible to Petra.

If we pay attention to the things Quist chooses to emphasize, we may notice that he seems to have arrived at a diagnosis of Petra's difficulties, even though he leaves it for the most part tacit. He selectively demonstrates aspects of the process that seem to be aimed at her specific problems. For example, she is disposed to deal with individual elements (to work "closely", as she says) rather than with the overall organization. So he focuses on establishing the basic geometry of the buildings on the site. She is hesitant to make the apparently arbitrary choices that can give meaning and value to her design by investing it with features she likes, features from which the basic idea can flow. Quist demonstrates for her a continuing oscillation between making such choices, on the one hand, and on the other, being rigorously obedient to their implications.

She is not adept at stringing out long and complex sequences of conditional moves and consequences. Quist (in his language of "you might . . ." and "this might happen here . . .") constructs for her a web of possible moves and consequences. But he also continually judges both what must now be done, given the implications of earlier moves, and what would be "good" or "nice" in the resulting effects. Through his dialectic

53

of positing, spinning out consequences, and evaluating, he enables the "whole idea" to take shape.

She is limited in her repertoire of norms and disciplines. Quist shows how she should allow herself to be influenced by many different domain-specific norms — the formal implications of chosen geometries, the use-related idea of "being one with the trees", the effects of orientation on the site, anthropometric standards, the feelingful meanings that may be attached to building elements, the uses compatible with various slopes, to name only a few. In the cases of the cafeteria and the auditorium, where Petra seems interested only in the purety of her hard-edged forms, Quist shows how it is possible to allow geometric forms to be "softened" and "broken open" by accommodation to norms derived from other domains.

She does not grasp certain relationships between features of orientation and form, matches of formal elements across vertical levels and the like. Quist gives her direct instructions about these matters and shows how she can apply them to the problem at hand.

What does Petra make of all this? Quist does not ask her, and she does not offer to tell him. If she remains confused about the meaning of "designing" in spite of Quist's demonstrations and reflections, neither we nor Quist can know it from the data available. But there is considerable evidence from other interviews and dialogues that many students at Petra's stage of development are thoroughly confused; indeed, they sometimes find the whole experience of the studio mysterious.

In Petra's studio, for example, in spite of the students' general admiration for Quist as practitioner and teacher, fully half of the group find it hard to grasp what he means by "thinking architecturally". Judith, a colleague of Petra's, has a jury in which the critic finally tells her,

> Unless you can begin to think of the problem architecturally
> ... you aren't going to find any way to proceed.

And Judith herself says, in a later interview,

> I began to realize that my approach wasn't architectural at all.

In another studio,[1] the studio master says of a student,

> Lauda is the hardest guy to deal with. Intelligent, articulate, comes up with something that works, but architecturally it's horrible. Now, what do I do? In a way, it's the kind of case which precipitates the weakest responses, because he has

not internalized some of the covert things . . . I think he should do something else. He is bright but totally unvisual. Within the frame of reference of a designing architect, he is totally misplaced . . . I wouldn't know what to do with him.

The teacher argues that because Lauda has not picked up the "covert things", the teacher does not (and cannot) know what to do with him. As for Lauda, he accepts but is rather bewildered by the demand that he perform according to standards that he finds alien and mysterious.

I think at times (the teacher) assumed a greater awareness on my part than I had . . . I wasn't doing it around my own standards. My standards were far surpassed . . . That's probably the key thing.

So, he says,

. . . (I want) to go out and learn first. I want to know what it is we are arguing about.

In yet another studio, a student who has not been singled out by his teachers as a problem, makes this poignant observation.

What we have is a very Kafkaesque situation where you really don't know where you are, and you have no basis for evaluation. You hang on the inflection of the tone of voice in your crit to discover if something is really wrong.[2]

So we must add the student's sense of confusion and mystery, at least in the early stages of the studio, to the features of design education I have already mentioned — the student trying to do something on her own; being unclear just what it is she is supposed to do; getting stuck; the studio master offering in demonstration, instruction, and reflection on the basis of his implicit diagnoses of her difficulties. These phenomena are not unique to Quist's dialogue with Petra, or even to Quist's studio as a whole, but are characteristic of most studio education. In order to make sense of them, we must identify the paradox with which design education necessarily begins. Then, as we see the learning/teaching predicament to which that paradox leads, we will recognise the implicit pedagogy of the studio. Whether we agree with it or not, we will find it intelligible.

Initially, the student does not and cannot understand what designing means. He finds the artistry of "thinking (and doing) like an architect" to be elusive, obscure, alien and mysterious. Conversely, the studio master realizes that the students do not initially understand the essential things and cannot be *told* those things at the outset, because the fundamental concepts of designing can be grasped only in the context of the doing —

only through the experience of designing. Further, at least some studio masters, like Lauda's, believe that, even in the experience of designing, some of the essential things must remain covert; one cannot explain them, the student must somehow internalize them. Hence the "Kafkaesque" situation in which the student must "hang on the inflection of the tone of voice in (his/her) crit to discover if something is really wrong".

In this sense, the design studio shares in a general paradox attendant on the teaching and learning of any really new competence or understanding. For the student seeks to learn things whose meaning and importance he cannot grasp ahead of time. He is caught in the paradox Plato describes so poignantly in his dialogue, *The Meno*. Here, just as Socrates induces him to admit that he hasn't got the least idea what virtue is, Meno bursts out with the question:

> But how will you look for something when you don't in the least know what it is? How on earth are you going to set up something you don't know as the object of your search? To put in another way, even if you come right up against it, how will you know what you have found is the thing you didn't know?[3]

The student does not yet know what he needs to know, yet knows that he needs to look for it. His instructor cannot tell him what he needs to know, even if *he* has words for it, because the student would not understand him.

The student is expected to find out for himself, to learn by doing. The studio seems to rest on the assumption that it is only in this way that he can learn. Though others may be able to help him, they can only do so as he begins to understand for himself the process he does not yet understand. And although they may help him, *he* is ultimately responsible. In a fundamental sense, he is expected to educate himself in designing.

Or as my friend, Tom Cowan put it,

> I like old Carl Gustave Jung best on education. You know that unlike Freud for whom psychoanalysis is a branch of the healing arts, Jung always insisted that it is a propadeutic, a branch of education. For him, education is what one does to and for one's self. Hence the universal irrelevance of all systems of education . . . This view forced me to distinguish education from training: Education — the self-learning process. Training — what others make you do — What are educational systems (so-called) *really* doing? For example,

law school, I discovered, primarily trains students to listen
... Law school *trains* people to think and talk the way the
rest of the profession does. What is its educational function
then? To drive you mad with its incessant drill to educate
yourself. The process appears terribly wasteful, yet some do
get educated. If the teacher had a big stick and hit you over
the head every time you tried to get him to educate you, the
thing would be done in less than a semester. It seems to me
that this is the Zen method of education, so of course, I
can't claim to have invented it.[4]

In the context of the studio, there is a double paradox: on the
one hand, the student cannot initially understand what he
needs to learn; on the other hand, he can only learn it by
educating himself, and he can only educate himself by
beginning to do it. This places the student in a predicament. He
is expected to plunge into the studio, trying from the very
outset to do what he does not yet know how to do, in order to
get the sort of experience that will help him learn what
"designing" means.

In this predicament, it is as though the teacher said:

I can tell you there is something you need to know, and I
can tell you that with my help you can probably learn it. But
I cannot tell you what it is in a way that you can now
understand. You must be willing, therefore, to undergo
certain experiences as I direct you to undergo them so that
you can learn what it is you need to know and what I mean
by the words I use. Then and only then can you make an
informed choice about whether you wish to learn this new
competence. If you are unwilling to step into this new
experience without knowing ahead of time what it will be
like, then I cannot help you. You must trust me.

As Quist puts it in an interview about his own studio, the
studio master asks the students to make a "willing suspension
of disbelief":

It has to be a kind of contract between the two — the
teacher must be open to challenge and must be able to
defend his position — the student, in turn, must be willing to
suspend his disbelief, to give the teacher's suggestion a
chance — to try the suggestion out. The student must be
willing to trust that the faculty member has a programmatic
intention which will be pre-empted or ruined by his
requiring full justification and explanation before anything

57

is done . . . a good student is capable of the willing suspension of disbelief.

Quist's phrase, "the willing suspension of belief", comes from Samuel Taylor Coleridge, who used it to describe the stance essential to our understanding of poetry. The poet tries to convey an esoteric experience, Coleridge thought. In order to read a poem in such a way as to grasp what the poet seeks to communicate, the reader must enter into a collaboration with him, willingly suspending his disbelief in utterances that seem to him mistaken, or even absurd. Only in this way can he allow the poem to do its work. Like the reader, the student is asked to will the suspension of disbelief in what the studio master has to tell him. He is not asked to will "belief", because he will not be able to believe until he understands, and he cannot understand until he has had the right sort of experience. The phrase also suggests that belief, when it comes, should be a matter of informed choice. Disbelief should be *suspended* until the student has access to the information on which to make a good decision. The student is asked to will *something*, however − to make an act of commitment to the enterprise on which he and the studio master will embark.

What makes this situation into a predicament for the student is that he, or she, is likely to feel that this commitment entails costs that cannot, in the nature of the case, be justified before the fact by their counterbalancing benefits. Perhaps the least of these is the fact that the student must forego, at least for a while, other opportunities for learning. More important is the fact that, as he enters into the new experience, he perceives himself to be at risk. He feels that he risks a loss of his sense of competence and control and, with these, a loss of confidence. For a time, at least, he will be swimming in unknown waters, without competence, without control, and indeed, without understanding.

He must temporarily abandon much that he already knows and values. If he comes to the studio with knowledge he considers useful for the task, he may well be asked to unlearn it, so as to open himself to new skills. If he comes with a perspective on what is valuable and important in design, he may be asked to put it aside in order to grasp a new perspective. Later in his studio education, or after it, he may be able to assess for himself the relative merits of his earlier and later perspectives, perhaps even to reconcile them. But in the early stages, he is unable to do this. And he may fear that, by a kind of insidious coercion or seduction, he may permanently lose what he already knows and values.

With his entry into a new experience in which he is relatively without competence and relatively without understanding of what he needs to learn, he will become significantly dependent upon his instructors. It is to them that he must look for understanding, direction, and help in the acquisition of competence. His willing suspension of belief is also a willing suspension of autocracy and distrust of dependency — all very much like becoming a child again. In such a predicament, he is likely to be vulnerable to anxiety.

The magnitude of the loss the student *feels* he is experiencing, the scope of the risk he feels he is taking, and the depth of his anxiety, have much to do with what he brings to the experience. If he has a relatively weak sense of his own competence and confidence, so that he is easily threatened by their temporary surrender, then his sense of loss, risk, and anxiety is likely to be high. Not so, if he is confident of his own competence and independence. Then a temporary surrender of control can seem innocuous. If he finds it easy to distrust those in authority, and see them as manipulating him — and if, more especially, he is unaware of these dispositions — then the willing suspension of disbelief will present him with grave and perhaps insuperable problems. Not so, if he needs reasons for distrusting others, rather than the reverse. And if he has learned to think *about* the process by which he restructures familiar meanings, then he will have a way of reflecting on the new experience of the studio; not so, if he has no concepts to describe what is happening to him.

In some respects, the studio master shares the student's predicament. Although he is likely to have greater understanding of the design process, and competence matched to his understanding, he knows that, in the first instance, he cannot convey these to his student. He knows that the student, like a postulant asked to make a leap of faith in order to attain belief, can get good reasons for taking action only by beginning to act. However much the studio master may dislike asking the student to make an initially unjustified surrender of autonomy and doubt — however much he may dislike having to abandon a view of the learning process as one in which he and the student participate as equal partners — his initial contract with the student, on which the effectiveness of design education depends, requires that the student make a willing suspension of disbelief, in spite of its perceived risks, and that the studio master invite him to do so.

To be sure, the learning contract is seldom explicit. Quist is rather an exception among studio masters in the degree to which he makes it into an object of reflection. Usually student and studio master simply find themselves in the situation described by the contract. And if they should happen to think about it later on, their reflections are likely to be embedded in the complex, multi-levelled process of communication in which, after the initial contract, the main work of the studio consists.

We can think of this process as one in which the participants send messages to one another and receive messages from one another. However, the transmission of their messages is not like a kind of telegraphy, in which signals (assumed to be inherently meaningful) are directly transferred from one participant to another. Rather the process is one of reciprocal *construction*. Each participant must construct for himself the meanings of the messages sent by the other, design messages whose meanings the other is likely to be able to construct, and test both that he has correctly constructed the other's meaning and that the other has correctly constructed his own. When this process works well, the result is a reliable convergence of meaning. So much of the studio shares with all human communication.

But the communication between student and studio master is, in several ways, exceptionally problematic.

First of all, messages usually refer, at once, to at least two kinds of things: the process of designing, and the process of learning to design. At the outset, the student is likely to be confused about both. A particular event, like Petra's desk crit, pertains to both processes and holds a potential for two interacting levels of confusion.

Second, messages about designing and learning to design are not primarily conveyed in the mode of talk but in the mode of action — through the studio master's demonstrations of designing and the student's efforts to design. Or, as in Quist's dialogue with Petra, the two kinds of actions provide a ground for talk about design. The fact that student and studio master communicate primarily by doing is essential to the effectiveness of their process. The student's success is measured, after all, not only by his ability to recognize and talk about good design, but by his ability to do it. On the other hand, this fact makes things, in some ways, more difficult. The student must be able to construct the meanings of the studio master's *actions* and must try to do this even though the studio master's meanings are likely to conflict, in ways he cannot anticipate, with his own. (The likelihood of their conflict underlies the need for an initial suspension of disbelief.) And the student cannot send messages through his own actions without making himself vulnerable to the perceived risks of confusion and failure.

Finally, the studio master's messages are often troubled by vagueness, ambiguity or obscurity. The most essential things are often those most likely to be initially unclear to the student, or even inexpressible in words. For example, in the design review we have examined, Quist devotes a great deal of effort to demonstrating the variety of design domains that must be taken into account in spinning out and evaluating the designer's choices. Nowhere, however, does he describe the system of design domains on which he draws; and even if he were to try to do so, some students would find this a point of extreme confusion — Lauda, for example, who can think only in terms of structure and technology. When Quist tells Petra that she must "draw and draw", he means drawing in the sense of drawn experiment. For some students, however, "drawing" can mean only the visual delineation of an already formed idea. When told to "draw and draw", they infer that their presentation lacks the polish of a professional presentation. Some students interpret Quist's use of "metaphor", which he intends to denote the image generative of a design, to mean a decorative attachment to an already established design. One student, having completed her basic drawing, suggests that in order to please her instructor she will "put in some metaphors".

The very notion of "thinking architecturally" can remain stubbornly ambiguous. A student has not really grasped the meaning of component design skills (analysing a program, making a *parti*, making a scale model) until he has experienced these processes in their interaction with one another in a whole process of design. Although the design master may break "thinking architecturally" into a set of independently learnable components, the student cannot understand and acquire each component skill, *in the sense in which "thinking architecturally" requires it,* until he has experienced that component in the context of the whole.

Similarly, vagueness and confusion may hover around such questions as the sources of evaluation judgments (the meanings underlying terms like "screwy", "nice", "horrible"), and the

61

degree of objective validity or relativity imputed to such judgments. On these matters, the instructor is often silent. As one student says,

> One of the things that really bugs me about architectural education is that a lot of things are really implicit, remain under the surface and are not talked about.

And such silences may themselves become sources of ambiguity, leaving the student free to believe, for example, that these things are obvious to everyone except him, or he is being challenged to find them out for himself, or this instructor cannot express them, or they are inexpressible or he, the student, has not learned to ask the right questions. The issue becomes crucial to a student when he is unable to grasp the underlying view of designing from which an instructor has criticized his work.

Although, in any particular interaction between student and studio master, the various types of ambiguity, vagueness or obscurity may not arise, the potential for them is inherent in the studio situation. The premise of the studio is that the student must begin to design before he knows what he is doing so that, in the light of this experience, the studio master's demonstrations and descriptions may begin to have meaning for him, and thereby help him to teach himself to design. But this virtuous circle depends on the capacity of student and instructor to search effectively for convergence of meaning about the "essential things". They must do this in spite of the potential for ambiguity, vagueness, or inexpressibility inherent in much of what they wish to communicate about. And they must do it in the context of a learning predicament which leads most students, at one time or another, to feel vulnerable and defensive.

Their search, and the strategies both parties may bring to it, will be the subject of the following section.

Part V: Coaching Artistry

As the student begins to design, even though he is not sure how to do it and does not know what he needs to know in order to learn to do it, the studio master may help him in two ways. He may demonstrate some part of the process he believes the student needs to learn, in which case he gives the student something to imitate. Or he may tell the student something about designing, general descriptions, specific instructions or criticisms, asking questions, suggesting that the student try various things — in all of which cases the student is expected to listen. Studio masters vary in their preferences for "showing" or "telling". Some refuse to draw for their students, fearing, perhaps, that the student's imitation will be blind and mechanical. Others will only draw, distrusting mere words as a vehicle of communication about something as inherently visual as designing. Some, like Quist, combine the two strategies.

Whatever the studio master's preference may be, two conditions must be met if the search for convergence of meaning is to be effective. The first is that the context must be one in which the student is actively engaged in trying to do something. The second is that demonstrating and imitating, telling and listening, must take the form of reciprocal reflection-in-action.

The studio master, when he works well, tries to figure out what the student understands, what his problems are about, what he needs to know, all of this from the main evidence of observation of the student's designing. The studio master's interventions, then, are experiments which test both the studio master's grasp of the student's understanding and the effectiveness of his intervention. In this way, the studio master reflects-in-action.

The student tries to grasp the meaning of the master's showing and telling and seeks to translate what he grasps into his own performance. Each such performance is an experiment which expresses the sense the student has made of what he has observed or heard and tests the means by which he translates

63

that sense into the task of designing. In this sense, the student reflects-in-action.

Studio master and student construct a dialogue in the media of words and performance. The student performs and presents the results of his performance; the master "reads" what he observes and tries to make interventions matched to the student's understanding and problems. The student tries to grasp the meaning of what the master has said and done, and to test his new understandings by translating them into a new performance. This process goes on continuously, within and across the design problems that make up the tasks of the studio. It is successful when it results in convergence of meaning, expressed in the student's ability to perform (in the particular context then appropriate) in a way that student and master can recognize as thinking and doing "like-an-architect". As the two persons approach convergence of meaning, their speech becomes more eliptical, they use shorthand in word and gesture to convey ideas that might seem complex to an outsider; they communicate with greater confidence; they finish one another's sentences, or leave sentences unfinished, confident that the other has grasped their meaning.

In the process of reciprocal reflection-in-action, several levels of learning are involved. As I have mentioned earlier, the student learns both about designing and about learning to design. For example, Petra learns about designing whatever she learns from Quist's demonstration (we do not know just what it is, although she does mention for example, she sees *why* a shape had seemed "intuitively wrong") and she also learns what to *expect* from a desk crit, what it expected of *her* in such an event, how she should present her inquiries and problems in order to get useful responses from Quist, what kinds of questions Quist is likely to ask that she might also come to ask herself, and the like.

Further, the student learns about design in the same process by which she learns about design*ing*. As we have seen, every experiment in designing involves judgments about what is "nice", "good", "interesting", "like what Aalto has done on occasion", or what is "horrible", "spoils the whole idea", "screwy". If the process works well, the student becomes aware that she must have likes and dislikes, values and preferences of her own, by which she judges the results of her design experiments. She learns how the studio master makes his judgments of design quality, and something of what enters into

64

those judgments, and she learns (with greater or lesser independence) to make her own judgments. She also learns to be attentive to certain norms of designing — for example, the norm of fidelity to the implications set up by one's prior moves — and to see the connections of those norms to the qualities she has learned to like in her own and other's work.

As student and studio master oscillate between descriptions of the qualities of designs and descriptions of designing, they also oscillate from one language to another. There is a language of appreciation (some elements of which I have cited above) and there is a language of performance which both Quist and Petra illustrate profusely in their dialogue. For example, Quist's "this (the dining room) might come down here to get summer sun here", "you must impose a discipline, you can always break it open later". Often Quist combines the two languages in the same sentence, as in "Then you might carry the gallery level through, and look down into here . . . which would be nice". In addition, there is (as I have already mentioned) language *about* designing, which we might think of as fragments of a theory about the design process, such as Quist's comments about working back and forth between unit and total, the need for subjection to a common geometry, "you will see that will be a common problem that will come up with everyone, either too much constraint or not enough". In the passages back and forth among the languages of appreciation, performance and theory of designing, student and studio master pass, in their reciprocal reflection-in-action, from one domain of attention to another, and from one level of description to another.

With this overview of the search for convergence of meaing, let us now examine more carefully the two main strategies of telling and listening, demonstrating and imitating. I shall first consider each of these separately, though, as we shall see further on, they are usually closely coupled and combined in actual practice. And I shall examine how they can work, even in the context of the learning paradox and predicament and the obstacles to communication I have previously described.

Telling and listening. The studio master's "telling" may take several forms,

— specific instructions about particular design tasks or situations, for example, the preparation of a site plan, how to assign uses appropriate to slopes of various grades, when to use cross-sectional drawings, elevations or plans,

— criticisms of the student's performance,

— suggestions of things the student needs to do next in a particular design task, like Quist's suggestion that Petra now work on the size of the "middle area", or calibrate the dimensions of her grid,

— proposals for new experiments the students ought to try,

— analysis of problems the student has encountered,

— general comments about good design, or about the process of designing,

— questions aimed at getting the student to pay attention to design domains previously ignored or to rethink the problem, or to become aware of important norms (drawing to scale, establishing orientation, considering the implications of a choice of geometry).

Most of these sorts of utterances are made in the context of the student's *doing.* They are made as the student is in the midst of a task (and perhaps stuck in it), or as the student is about to begin a task, or thinking back on a task just completed, or rehearsing in imagination a task she may perform in the future. Clearly, the things the studio master says in contexts like these have a potential for communication to the student that they would not have in other contexts. Once the student has begun to design, the studio master can begin to communicate what designing is about. But there is no magical dividing line between the studio and the world outside it. The student does not suddenly understand, when she steps into the studio, what she had found obscure while she remained outside it. Nevertheless, master and student can begin their reflective dialogue about design, designing and learning to design, once the student has begun to design. What happens to make this possible?

In the context of action, both the studio master's telling and the student's listening, take on new potentials for effectiveness. These have to do with the way in which the student can pay attention to what she hears, with the way in which the student's designing provides a source of feedback about the sense she has made of what she has heard, and with the special demands both parties place on verbal descriptions when they must be translated into action.

When Quist tells Petra, for example, about placing administration, kindergarten, and gym on the site, she listens to him in a special way because she is engaged in trying to place them on the site. She listens rather as we listen to directions telling us how to get somewhere when we are the ones who will have to drive. It is one thing to listen to a description of a process as though it were mere information divorced from action; another, to listen to it with the understanding that it is an instruction for the performance of a task; and still another, to listen to it as an instruction we must presently try to follow. In the last case, which might be called "operational attention", we listen with a readiness to translate what we hear into action which means that we must construct its meaning in our own performance. In this case, unless the instruction is one we already know how to follow, it is always incomplete. There are always *gaps* between the description of action contained in the instruction and the kind of description from which we can act. We become aware of them only when we try to act from the instruction or imagine what it would be like to put it into action. We then put a different kind of demand both on the instruction and on our understanding of it, namely that the discovered gaps are ones we can figure out how to fill.

The gaps between instruction and performance are of several kinds.

The instruction may not have *appropriate specificity*. It may not be specific enough, or may not have the right sort of specificity, for the student to be able to apply it to the situation at hand. In order to follow Quist's advice to "draw and draw, in order to calibrate the grid", Petra must know how to carry out the drawing experiments involved in such a calibration. She must know, for example, how to test a particular choice of dimension for its impacts on access to buildings, circulation, and fit to the contours of the slope. Quist may give her examples of what it might mean to test a grid's dimensions in these ways, but his examples may not be matched to the particular problem Petra feels she is having or to what she already knows how to do. He may discover this through her questions, or through observation of her attempts to follow his instructions. In order to get to the level of appropriate specificity, for her in this instance, he must say enough of the right sort of thing (right for her sense of problem and for her existing know-how) without trying to say everything. He must become aware that some of the things he takes for granted are just the things that give her the greatest difficulty.

The instruction may be *ambiguous*. It may have the peculiar sorts of ambiguity characteristic of the language of designing (some of which I have described in the previous section), or it may have the general kind of ambiguity common to all instructions. With respect to the latter, one need only try to follow someone's directions for getting to a place; "take the first left after the lights" may turn out, for example, to mean "take the first *paved* left" — the dirt road immediately after the lights was not meant to count! In such a case, as in the case of Quist's instructions to Petra, the active listener, trying to translate the instruction into a competent performance, discovers ambiguities of which the giver of the instructions is unaware. For the instructor, the instruction is not ambiguous; he has already done all the necessary gap-filling and takes for granted the tacit know-how that went into it. For the active listener, the discovered ambiguity is a problem to be solved — alone, or with the instructor's help.

The instruction may be *novel*, in the sense that it refers to things, procedures, or qualities that are not yet in the listener's repertoire. Petra may not be able to follow Quist's advice about "being one with the trees" because this idea is strange to her, not yet among her "things to think with".

The instruction may contain intended meanings that *conflict* with the meanings the listener constructs for it. The student may not perceive an instruction as ambiguous, for example — may think that he "gets it" — and may, nevertheless, perform it in a way that reveals to the instructor a meaning incongruent with his own. This is what happens, for example, when a student decides to "put in some metaphors".

In all four kinds of cases — inappropriate specificity, ambiguity, novelty, conflict of meaning — the student discovers, or reveals, gaps between instruction and performance which become visible only when there is an attempt to translate instruction into action. For both student and studio master, the instruction then becomes subject to the demand that it be translatable into action — and, indeed, into an action of the sort the instructor had in mind. Moreover, such gaps are revealed in a context in which they can be filled, either through the student's private experimenting, or through his dialogue (drawing and explaining) with the instructor.

And here it is important to notice a further sense in which the context of doing makes it possible for student and studio master to begin to understand one another. When the student is engaged in designing, his performance can serve, for the instructor and for himself, as evidence of the meanings he has constructed for the instructor's descriptions. His performance is a text in which it is possible to read his understandings. Seeing what the student has drawn, the studio master can realize that the student thinks "drawing to scale" means using a ruler. The student can realize that he does not really know what it means to "calibrate the grid". The student's attempts to translate descriptions into performance can reveal unanticipated gaps in description, indicate incongruities of meaning not previously suspected, show that the student has a problem different from the one the instructor had in mind. And on the basis of such feedback, the instructor can invent what he ought to say next.

The student's attempted performance is just as much an utterance as the instructor's attempted description. Both are experimental moves in a process of reflection-in-action.

For the student, every attempt at translating instruction into action is an experiment that tests his construction of the instructor's meaning. He asks himself, in effect, have I got it right? Do I understand what he is talking about? Does it make sense to me? Can I do it? For the studio master, every utterance is the output of an attempt to read the test of the student's performance for its content of understanding and problems. What he chooses to say to the student tests his reading. But it also tests his answers to other questions, any or all of which may be alive for him in the dialogue. He may ask himself, for example, what kind of language will best match this student's problem or understanding? What Tolstoy says of the teacher of reading holds also for the teacher of designing:

Every individual must, in order to acquire the art of reading in the shortest possible time, be taught quite apart from any other, and therefore there must be a separate method for each. That which forms an insuperable difficulty to one does not in the least keep back another, and vice versa. One pupil has a good memory, and it is easier for him to memorize the syllables than to comprehend the vowellessness of the consonants; another reflects calmly and will comprehend a most rational sound method; another has a fine instinct, and he grasps the law of word combination by reading whole words at a time.

The best teacher will be he who has at his tongue's end the explanation of what it is that is bothering the pupil. These explanations give the teacher the knowledge of the greatest possible number of methods, the ability of inventing new methods and, above all, not a blind adherence to one method but the conviction that all methods are one-sided, and that the best method would be the one which would

> answer best to all the possible difficulties incurred by a
> pupil, that is, not a method but an art and talent.
> ... Every teacher must ... by regarding every imperfection
> in the pupil's comprehension, not as a defect of the pupil,
> but as a defect of his own instruction, endeavour to develop
> in himself the ability of discovering new methods ...

Like Tolstoy's teacher, the studio master may call in different
ways on the elements of his repertoire in order to match his
descriptions to the particular student's way of understanding,
or he may invent new interventions on the spot. Similarly, he
may choose to say different things depending on his reading of
the student's particular design situation. For example,

— He may ask a question aimed at directing the student's
attention to a new aspect of the situation: "Why does the
administration belong here? What if you opened up the space
here?"

— He may ask a question that contains within it an idea the
student may not yet have entertained: "How will you mark
these level differences?" (where the student has not yet noticed
that there are differences to be marked).

— He may give the student a very concrete instruction that
contains implicitly, a deeper meaning. He might say, for
example, "Why don't you see what it looks like in cross-
section?", hoping that the student will notice, then, that the
gallery (to return to Petra's drawing) is more than a vehicle for
circulation. The hope is that the student will translate from the
concrete instruction to an unstated, essential meaning. In effect,
the studio master then tries to get the student to put herself in a
position to see something that she might not see if it were
stated in general terms. In a similar spirit, a piano teacher
might say, "You should change the fingering here", meaning,
"There is really a new phrase which you must begin here".

— He may pick up the exact words with which a student has
described her intention, developing them, however, in a
direction different from the one the student had in mind, as
when Quist says, "It is a general pass-through that anyone has
the liberty to pass through, but it is not a corridor ..."

— He may try to find a concrete image, accessible to this
student, which carries a complex network of associations. Thus
Quist speaks of a "garden, a soft back area to these (hard-
edged forms)." In an analogous vein, a skiing instructor might
say, "You should *plant* the pole here!"

Just as the instructor may vary his strategies of description, according to his reading of the particular student or design problem, so he may vary the timing of what he says, or the manner in which he says it. He makes judgments about a student's need to know something just now, or about her readiness to hear it. He may treat one student with great gentleness and indirection, barely hinting at issues which would call for new directions of work. With another, he may be direct, aggressive, challenging. In Quist's studio, some of the variations in student response to him may reflect the different sides of himself that he chooses to present to different students.

As he selects strategies of description from his repertoire, or invents them, the studio master engages in reflection-in-action. He reflects on the student's performance, makes an on-the-spot experiment responsive to his reading, and judges his experiment by its impact on the student's further performance − which derives, in turn, from the student's on-the-spot construction of the instructor's meaning. The process is one of reciprocal reflection-in-action. And in this process, the student's performance is pivotal. It tests and reveals, at once, the instructor's reading of the student's situation, the appropriateness of the invervention selected, and the sense the student has made of it.

To be sure, the process need not be self-conscious. Studio master and student need not reflect on their reflection-in-action but may pass spontaneously from one reading and response to another, without a "stop and think". But if they do stop and think − perhaps when they feel their dialogue is not working − then they may become aware of the on-line experimentation and reflection in which they have been engaging and the tacit assumptions and strategies they have been employing.

Demonstration and imitation. A great deal of what Quist does in his dialogue with Petra consists not in "telling" but in showing. Starting with the givens of her design situation, and the big problems she has described, he gives her a demonstration of a version of the sort of design process she has already tried (stutteringly, as Quist says) to carry out.

How shall we describe the intention with which Quist makes this demonstration? Clearly, he intends to show her something so that she will understand it. But, equally clearly, he intends her to go on and do something like it. "You should go on", he says, "you are going to make it!" Quist has demonstrated how one might go about building this diagramatic process of

71

designing the layout of the buildings on the site so that Petra can proceed to imitate it — to imitate, that is, not the details or the mechanics of the process but its essential features. And Petra seems to accept the demonstration in the spirit Quist intends. She seems to feel that he has made clear to her why she was stuck, why certain things had seemed to her to be "intuitively wrong"' and she seems to attribute to herself, as Quist attributes to her, a capacity to go on and do as he has done.

In a more general sense, the studio master uses his capacity to demonstrate aspects of designing as a way of helping the student to grasp what designing means, what she needs to learn that she may not, at the outset, realize she needs to learn. And when he does, he attributes to her — as part of what she already knows how to do — the capacity for a certain kind of imitation.

At first glance, there is nothing strange in this. Imitation is practiced, virtually universally, as a way in which one individual learns to do what another individual already knows how to do. Children learn to play by imitating other children. They learn to enter the adult world by imitating the adults around them. Adults learn sports, games, working skills, the business of everyday life, by imitating those who are already proficient. It is true that for adults the idea of imitation has negative connotations (we shall have more to say about these later on); still, most adults continually engage in imitation and generally take the process for granted. They may not like the idea of imitating someone else, but this does not prevent them from doing it and considering it an obvious thing to do. The sense of obviousness dissolves, however, the moment we consider imitation more closely.

For imitation is not simply the reproduction of an observed behaviour. It is a complex process of *construction,* in which the student must form an idea of what is essential in the demonstration — those aspects of it that are to be imitated. And, in complementary fashion, the student reveals by her performance what she perceives as essential in the demonstration.

Imitation need not, and usually does not, proceed through an intermediate verbal description of the action to be imitated. The constructive performance usually comes first; verbal description usually comes, if at all, when the imitator reflects on what she has done. And often, a verbal description, when it

72

is given, seems an inadequate account of what the performer has actually done. Imitation involves a process of seeing one thing as another and doing as another person has done, without necessarily being able to say in what respects the two performances are alike. Further, the imitator may transfer what she has made of an observed performance to a new situation, one both similar and different from the first, and transform her performance to fit the new situation.

Petra may imitate Quist's demonstration of the laying out of school buildings on the site, producing a new layout of her own which is, nevertheless, similar in certain essential respects to Quist's. Then, when she goes on to the next design problem, she may proceed in the diagrammatic phase essentially as Quist showed her in the case of the school — this time, however, entirely different conditions of site and program. It is important to note here, first, that Petra may transfer the essentials of Quist's way of handling the diagrammatic phase of design without replicating the details of his first demonstration (indeed, as the famous tale of Epaminondas reminds us, to be unable to do this is to embody a classic type of stupidity); and second, Petra may succeed in translating and transferring what she observes of Quist's demonstration without being able to give a good verbal description of the essential thing that she has picked up and carried over into the new problem.

To imitate, at this higher level of apprehension and performance, is to take the demonstration as an exemplar or precedent for further action. It involves *seeing* the later problem *as* the earlier one and *doing* in the later *as* Quist has done in the earlier. It is, in effect, a version of the process of generative metaphor. Carrying what she has made of Quist's demonstration over into a new problem, Petra would construct in her new performance an embodiment of her grasp of the essentials of his. One might say that she tries to understand him by performing essentially like him. And she may reveal in her performance more or less of what he regards as essential to his. Her performance is, in this sense, a source of feedback about her grasp of his meanings and a continuation, in action, of their dialogue.

The things Quist and Petra say to one another take on a special significance when they are uttered in the context of imitative construction. Quist's language of designing — his combination of drawing and talking, as in "If this is the gully

and this, the hill, then there might be a bridge here . . ." —
makes manifest and understandable, for purposes of
understanding and imitation, what would be opaque if it
consisted in drawing alone. His language about designing — as
in his advice to "impose a discipline" or "work back and forth
between unit and total" — take on special significance because
they are intended to "coach" Petra in her efforts at imitation.

Although Petra need not reflect on the process in which she
engages when she imitates Quist, her ability to do so may
enhance her powers of imitation, in the sense of enabling her to
grasp and correct what she, or Quist, sees as a failure to
translate the essentials into action. And her ability to reflect, in
the course of imitation, gives her, as well, a greater freedom to
choose — to criticize and to retain, or reject, elements of her
imitation of Quist.

Such a process of reflective imitation may be divided into
several "moments". These are usefully distinguished from one
another, even though they may not be cleanly separated from
one another in the actual doing:

(1) *She perceives what he does.*

She recognizes it, in the sense of grasping the essential
features that she will shortly embody in her own designing.

(2) *She does as she has seen him do.*

This is a multi-levelled process of translation and
construction. She must first of all transpose the pattern she sees
as an outsider of observer into the pattern she feels as a
producer of the action. She must transform the theme of the
action she perceives in this context into a new variation to be
produced in a new context. She may "get it" more or less. One
way in which she may fail to get it, at first, is that she may
replicate superficial details — mannerisms — of Quist's
performance; her imitation may be merely mechanical.

(3) *She reflects on her performance.*

She reflects on his doing and hers by looking to see in what
ways she has produced in her situation what is essential in the
relation of his performance to his situation. This is one of the
points in the process where she may fall into confusion —
discovering, for example, that she has failed to construct what
is essential in his performance. Note, too, that she may be
unable at this point to say what it is that she has failed to get.

She may then seek, with Quist's help, perhaps, to reflect in a
further sense, trying to put into words what is like and unlike in
the two performances. And her reflections on her efforts at

imitation may be joined to reflection on the tacit knowing-in-action that she finds already embedded in her own performance. What she already knows and does spontaneously, without conscious intention, may stand as an obstacle to her imitative construction of his performance. Through her reflections, then, she may analyse and correct her performance, bringing it closer to what she perceives as essential in his; or she may succeed in drawing her earlier knowing-in-action into a new integration with his. In this process, Quist may help her by his explicit reflections on his own performance. At the same time, Petra's may serve as a kind or mirror for Quist, helping him to gain a better understanding of what he is really doing.

Petra may reflect, in the still further sense of critical evaluation of what she "gets" when she gets it. How does she like what she does when she does as he does? (This is the point at which, she can "always break it open"). What does she choose to keep, to give up, or to change?

(4) *She internalizes the performance, in its essentials, making it her own.*

She "goes over it" until she can perform in this way intuitively, spontaneously, no longer in the mode of imitative construction of his actions but by having brought this way of performance into her own repertoire.

The entire process of reflective imitation is an important part of what students already know how to do when they enter the studio, or an important part of what they learn to do when they increase their ability to learn to design. Students who are not gifted with this antecedent competence must learn it in the very same process by which they try to learn the new process of designing — learning to engage in reflective imitation as they learn designing through reflective imitation. Moreover, they may need to unlearn other ways of learning which interfere with this one. Their success in building a capacity for reflective imitation greatly influences, as we shall see, the learning outcomes of their studio experience.

The ladder of reflection. In the actual exchange of student and studio master, the process of telling and listening, demonstrating and imitating, are variously combined and interwoven.

— the studio master, while demonstrating, reflects on his own performance,

— the student, presenting her drawing, reflects on the steps she has taken and the problems she has experienced,

— the master describes and criticizes the student's performance (as in Quist's, "sort of what you have here", or "what you have done stutteringly . . ."),

— the master instructs the student to carry out a particular task (as in Quist's comment that Petra should draw the gallery in section),

— the master proposes experiments for the student to try, the student tries them, and the master joins the student in reflecting on the results of the trials,

— the student reflects aloud on the difficulties she experiences as she tries such an experiment, questions the master about a gap she has found in his instructions,

— the master demonstrates the new procedure he has advised her to try, or demonstrates both correct and incorrect ways of executing the procedure.

Telling, demonstrating, questioning, translating into performance, reflective imitation, criticism, all may be "chained" in various combinations, in such a way that the later events of doing, telling, translating and reflecting build on earlier ones. The context of such a dialogue is set by the fact that the student is engaged in a design task, or has just finished one, or is just about to engage in one. Moves in the dialogue are executed in a variety of media and languages. The master may draw, talk, combine drawing and talking, point to features of the student's drawing or to features of his own or some other drawing or slide meant to function as precedent. He may employ, in various combinations, the language of appreciation, performance, or theory.

Each party engages in designing, or in helping the other to design, and each engages in communication with the other about the designing in which they are engaged.

Each party engages, in several senses, in on-the-spot experimentation and reflects, in several senses, on his own and the other's experimentation. Some experimenting has the function of testing what the other means by what he says or does, or what the other makes of what one says or does. Reflection, in one's own interventions or on the other's punctuates the process of experimentation and contributes to the search for reliable convergence of meaning.

Designing is itself, as we have seen, a process of reflective conversation with the materials of the design situation. Draped over this process, as it were, is the reciprocal reflection-in-action of student and studio master. In this process, each party makes utterances, in words or actions, which are experiments in communication; he reflects on what the other makes of them, tries to test his perceptions of the other's messages, constructs meaning for them, and tries to test the reliability of his construction.

We can think of this process in terms of the metaphor of a *ladder of reflection*. There are levels, or "rungs", of reflection, which refer to the level below and serve as objects of reflection at the level above.

The base, or "ground" level consists of the substantive phenomena of the design process (in our example, the contours of the slope, the grid, the problem of circulation and access, the level differences, the meaning of the gallery).

One level up, there is reflection on the action of designing. This may take the form of advice about, or enunciation of principles for, designing (as in Quist's comment that "at this point I wouldn't worry about the roof"). But reflection at this level may also take the form of reflection on the knowing-in-action embedded in one's designing — not "what I believe to be true about designing" but the know-how implicit in my actual designing. Here, the designer may address questions such as these: What made me decide to put the turning circle here? What domains am I treating as relevant here? What implications flow from the moves I have made so far? How am I framing the problems of my design at this point?

At the next level, student or studio master may reflect on the meaning of the other's words or actions.

The student may ask, for example, What is the essential meaning in the demonstration Quist has just given? What does he really mean by describing the gallery as "in a minor way the major thing?" And he may then seek to test his understanding by eliciting the master's further reflection on what he has said or done, or by trying to translate it into his own performance. The testing process may be private, in which case the student explores whether he can do as the master has done, compares his performance with the master's instructions, sees whether he likes what he gets when he does this, or considers whether he gets something essentially similar to the master's product. The testing process may be interactive. The student may try to restate what the master has said, or describe what the master has done, or ask for criticisms of his own performance.

The master may ask, for example, What does he really want to know when he asks this question? What are the

77

understandings he reveals, the problems he shows, by what he does? What kinds of instructions or demonstrations would really help him now? What way of telling him, or showing him, is most likely to reach him? At what point is he likely to plug in? Reflections of this sort lead the master to try descriptions in the form of instructions, suggestions, or theory about the process in which the student is engaged. The master may then try to test, in the privacy of his own mind, the effects of his interventions on the student, observing what the student says at that point, his non-verbal; cues, or his performance following the master's intervention. Or, like Quist with Petra, the master may *not* try to test what the student makes of his intervention. Or he may ask the student to join him in the testing process by asking him what he has made of what the master said or did, or by eliciting the student's reflections on his further designing.

These levels and kinds of reflection may be conceived as a ladder, in the sense that the higher rungs are about, and in response to, what happens at the lower ones. When something is perceived, by either part, as "not working" at a lower level, it is possible to "climb up" to reflect (and action) at the next level. When something seems not to be working in the designing, student or studio master may climb up to reflect about designing. When something is not working in the communication about designing, as either party sees it, he may climb up a "rung" of reflection on that communication — as in the example of the master's reflection of his own demonstration.

The two examples that follow are illustrations of the operation of such a ladder of reflection. The first is drawn from a third-year design studio; the second, from a master class in violin — not an example of studio teaching, but one that shows an important similarity between the coaching processes that may be found in studio and conservatory settings. In both examples, the coach displays, in his reflection-in-action, an awareness both of the problem of helping the student to acquire new strategies of performance and, at the same time, the problem of constructing an interaction with the student that reduces the likelihood that the student will become defensive.

In the first example, the studio master, Danny, has assigned the problem of designing a field school — a training school located in a rural setting. One student, Elena, came in with what she subsequently described as a "school solution" (nobody had asked her to do this; it was what she had tacitly

78

assumed the situation called for). Danny described it as an arrangement of banana-shaped buildings in a field, a kind of motel. He asked her whether she *liked* what she had done. She said, no, she didn't, but she thought it was what would be called for in the studio. He asked her what she would *like* such a school to be. The question took her by surprise. It has not occurred to her that what she liked would matter. After some thought, she said she would like the field school to be "hidden", she would like it to be "one with nature", and she would like it to stimulate social activity. With a few quick sketches, Danny showed her several different ways in which she might consider producing the qualities she liked. She went home, and over a two-week period of intense immersion, she came up with a series of lively, evocative drawings in which, indeed, she had found ways of "hiding" the school in its natural setting and constructing arrangements conducive to social interaction. In the workshop I conducted, where Danny gave this example, the student was present. Although the event had occurred eight years earlier, she had kept all her drawings and remembered every detail of the interaction.

The second example I've drawn from is a master class in violin. Dorothy DeLay of the Julliard School (famous now as Yitzhak Perlman's coach) sat listening to a series of performances by gifted young performers. Each student had prepared a piece and each performed it in turn, uninterruptedly, sometimes for as long as twenty minutes, while Miss DeLay sat impassively, listening. After each student played, she would say something like, "That was wonderful, sugar", and then would do something quite particular to *that* performer. Sometimes, her comments would have to do with intonation (she kept an electronic tuning fork for cases such as this), sometimes with the technical details of fingering or bowing, sometimes (in the case of a German student who listened precariously to one side) with posture. The only time she talked about specifically *musial* issues was to a young Chilean woman who had played with outstanding musicality — not a virtuoso stint but the first movement of a Brahms sonata. Dorothy asked that student to play what she felt to be the main themes of the movement. The student obliged by playing first one, then another. The third one played, Dorothy observed, seemed to be not a new theme but a variation of the first. She asked then whether there wasn't something "transitional". The student found it, played it, and agreed that it was, indeed, a third theme.

Dorothy asked her, then, how she would describe the qualities of these themes? The student thought for a moment, then offered the view that the first was "lively", the second "stormy", the third "reflective". Dorothy said, "Suppose we wanted to accentuate the liveliness of the first, how would we do it?" She put her head in her hands, thinking about the problem. Then she said, "There's an up-beat that goes to a resting place, ta-dum. Perhaps you could really *spring* off of it, and land on the next — ta-*dum*. The student tried it, produced the effect, liked it. Then, "How about the third, how woud you make it really 'reflective'?" the student seemed puzzled, then proposed a fingering and bowing that gave a very gently performance of the figure. Dorothy said, "Yes, you could do that. Or you could also *restrict* the bowing," and she mimed what she meant. The student tried it. Yes, that would work, too. "Which do you think you'll use?" Dorothy asked. The student seemed puzzled again. "I'm not sure, I'll have to think about it." Dorothy sat back, obviously pleased.

I'm struck by several features common to both of these examples. First, both coaches asked their students to reflect on their feelings about what they are doing. In both cases, they made it legitimate for the student to like or dislike something; and in both, they invited the student to reflect on and describe the qualities of what was liked. Then, these descriptions were taken as the materials of a problem: how to *produce* what was liked? This was taken as a problem for the student *and* instructor. Both parties stood, as it were, in front of the same problem. Suggestions were made as to ways in which the described qualities might be produced. The coach seemed to be inviting the student to join her in the process of experimentation — indeed, if anything was being taught by demonstration, not by description, it was the idea of practice as experimentation. And the relationship that had been constructed was not that of performer and critic but that of partnership in the setting and experimental solving of a problem.

The image of the ladder suggests that one can climb it at will, and that each rung presents a degree of difficulty more or less the same as the others. However, particular "rungs" may present difficulties peculiar to themselves. Either student or studio master, for example, may find it difficult to reflect on what he takes for granted; it is not easy to reflect on what one may not be aware of knowing already. Some things — the "covert things" — may present themselves to either party as inexpressible, therefore not susceptible to clarification by reflection. On the other hand, the experience of inexpressibility may have to do with the student, or studio master's willingness to try to put things in words, or in words and drawing combined. Whether a thought about designing is expressible may depend, to some extent, on the individual's skill in expressing it, in turn a function of practice in such expression. Belief in the centrality of "covert things" may help to keep them covert, contributing to a mystification of design. But it may also be true that, for a given student at a particular time, nothing the studio master does or says can succeed in communicating a certain essential idea. The question of inexpressibility, then, is perhaps best treated as an open question, to be explored through experiment in each interaction. The ladder of reflection would then function as a structure within which such explanations might proceed.

The image of a ladder of reflection suggests an explicit ordering of reciprocal reflection whereas interactions between student and studio master usually unfold in the studio in a more or less spontaneous, intuitive way. Yet, as protocol of student/studio master interactions suggest, both parties do sometimes reflect, individually (or with peers) and with one another, on their efforts at communication. Studio masters and students differ from one another in how much of this sort of thing they do, how they do it, and how well they do it. And both parties, students and instructors, who are frequently troubled by failures in the search for convergence of meaning or intrigued by unexplained successes, often express interest in shared reflection on the process in which they are engaged and enter rather readily, at least in my experience, into collective efforts to improve it. The ladder of reflection may serve both as an explicit model of a process that is usually casual and spontaneous, and as a basis for the more deliberate and systematic reflections that some participants in the studio wish to undertake.

Conclusion. The process I have described is one in which both parties engage in certain kinds of work — the work of designing, and the work of communication about (and through) designing. We may call these sorts of work "cognitive", not in the sense that they consist only of thinking but in the sense that they call for certain kinds of intelligence. The effectiveness of the joint search for convergence of meaning depends on studio master and student being able to perform certain kinds of tasks.

For the studio master, the tasks include demonstrating and telling, in all the variations I have described; reading the student's understanding and problems, as revealed in performance; reflection on one's own knowing-in-action; and reading and testing the impact on the student of what one says and does. The student is called upon to educate himself in designing, both through reflection on his own efforts to design and through active listening and reflective imitation, reflection on his own knowing-in-action, and testing of his grasp of the studio master's meaning. Moreover, student and studio master are called upon to perform these tasks in various reciprocal interactions with each other.

But it is not enough for student and studio master to have the competences essential to such cognitive work. They must also choose to think about such tasks and, by engaging them, build their competences for them. Their stance toward one another, and toward the work they share, must be conducive to reciprocal reflection-in-action.

Part VI: Conclusion — What can be Learned from the Experience of the Architectural Studio

Architecture is a profession rooted in the artistry of designing — a process that is not wholly mysterious but rather, at least in part, describable. Competent practitioners can learn to reflect on their own architectural inquiry. They can, in varying degrees, discover and describe how they function as on-line researchers, on-the-spot experimenters. They can articulate features of their reflective conversations with the materials of a design solution and can indicate how these may be rigorous in their own way. Indeed, in the architectural studio some competent instructors do engage in such reflection.

The artistry of designing is similar in important ways to the artistry sometimes exhibited in other fields of professional practice — especially in the indeterminate zones of complexity, uncertainty, uniqueness and value-conflict. But the normative curriculum of the professional schools has been selectively inattentive to artistry. The architectural studio is intrinsically interesting to those schools because it represents a tradition of education for reflection-in-action — for problem-setting, *ad hoc* theory-building, on-the-spot experimenting — that other professions are learning increasingly to value.

Insofar as other professions seek to reform their schools by combining their normative curriculum with education in artistry, they have much to learn from the traditions of studio education in architecture. And to the extent that architects — practitioners and studio masters — choose to reflect on their own performance, they are potential leaders in that much-needed process of reform. To the extent that they choose to do this, moreover, they are more likely to be successful in constructing a viable and vital future for their own schools.

What architectural education can learn from reflection on its own traditions

Architectural education faces challenges and predicaments, new and old. As it seeks to respond to a changing practice, in which architects function increasingly in new roles, it must make room for the introduction of new fields of knowledge — especially the new bodies of applied science, technology and technique that are essential to the management of complex design teams. How will these new materials enter the curriculum? How will they be married to the traditions of studio education? How will they be taught? About these matters, architecture has a choice. It is not as yet encumbered with a great deal of professional knowledge of dubious utility, taught in a way that obscures its origins in inquiry. As it strives to make something new, it is relatively free of the need to reform already existing patterns of teaching. On the other hand, architectural education is still caught up in the pluralism that has characterized the field at least since the early decades of this century and in conflicting views of itself as a social function or as an art. Response to the new challenge is unlikely to be effective unless it also takes account of the familiar predicament.

Responding to pluralism

The prevailing response to architectural pluralism — the babble of voices claiming to represent Architecture — has been that of the supermarket. Some schools have tended to organize themselves around the work of a particular "great man", embodying his conception of the practice, his images of desirable buildings, his view of the design process. Taken together, schools of this sort constitute a supermarket of education opportunities. By a decision to enter one of them, the student commits himself — at least for the duration of his education — to a particular school of architectural thought. Other schools have tried for internal diversity, creating within themselves the microworlds of several architectural movements. In both cases, the work of choice or synthesis is left to the student, who is perhaps least able to carry it out. As we have seen, the variety of architectural visions and styles creates for students a dilemma of objectivity. But are they to make sense of competing claims to architectural excellence? What grounds of validity can they attribute to them? Should they treat the competing schools of thought as mere expressions of taste and fashion or as claims to knowledge? And if the latter, on what basis are the claims to be evaluated? Even if the competition among architectural schools of thought is not objectively resolvable, are there still criteria for the evaluation of competent execution of the design process?

When architectural designing is understood along the lines of my analysis of Quist's demonstration, it can be evaluated *within* the framework of the designer's appreciative system, independent of anyone's mere think-so. When designing is considered as a kind of experimentation, undertaken within the virtual world of sketch-pad or scale model, it can be assessed as relatively competent or incompetent according to several criteria. Does the designer's web of moves meet minimal conditions for experimentation? Has the designer set problems she can solve? Has she created something she likes, or something out of which she can make something she likes? Has she succeeded in combining elements and values drawn from a variety of domains of relevance into a visible coherence which is also comprehensible to others? When the designer encounters a conflict of frames, frame-shift can result from an inquiry grounded in strongly held but conflicting values — where the conflict of values cannot be resolved except by a shift of frame. Criteria such as these are already embodied, I believe, in some of the existing practice of studio masters, and often enter into the dialogue between studio master and student. Judgments are made and reasons for them are given, debated and tested. Design discourse can aspire to a kind of objectivity — always relative to the appreciative system of the designer. Paradoxically, the kind of objectivity attainable in design inquiry depends upon the designer's preferences, however shared or idiosyncratic these may be. What is crucial, from the point of view of the student's dilemma of objectivity, is that the usually tacit bases for judgment be made more nearly explicit and more clearly related to the appreciative systems on which they depend. Such systematic self-reflection is equally important to the architectural educators' effort to meet the newer challenges facing them.

Emergent roles and field of knowledge

Such newly visible roles as design team manager, architect-developer, and architect-as-enabler, create demands for specialized bodies of knowledge and competence which reveal the limits of traditional architectural education and pose new challenges to curriculum design.

In various contexts of practice, architects are being called upon to display either expert knowledge or appreciation of fields such as these:

— ecology, climate and microclimate, soil mechanics, site planning, regional economics and, in general, bodies of knowlege relevant to the natural, made-made or made-influenced environments for building,

— the techniques of project management and the

interpersonal competences central to leadership in the conduct of interdisciplinary teams,

— real estate development, building finance, and building management,

— the study of the cultural context of those who will use the structures or inhabit the environment designed,

— the institutional and political contexts of design and building; negotiation with stakeholders in the design and building process,

— the conservation and rehabilitation of buildings and the built environment,

— the internal environment of buildings, including acoustic and thermo-dynamic properties,

— skills in post-occupancy evaluation and the management of participation in design and building.

It is not difficult to identify some of the questions posed by the expanding horizon of fields of knowledge thought to be relevant to architecture. Which of these should be taught in school? Which left to practice? Who should learn what, and when? More significantly, perhaps, we can identify a dilemma facing schools. Recognizing the increasing importance of the new (and especially, the technical) fields of knowledge to the education it must provide, architecture may try to incorporate them in a way that imitates technical education in other fields, thereby turning its back on the tradition of the studio. Or, out of a wish to remain true to a certain view of that tradition — and to the image of the architect as form-giver — architecture may turn its back on the rising demands for technical education. Either response is likely to carry a high price; in the first case, a loss of architecture's unique contributions to education; in the second, an increasing divergence from the demands of practice.

It seems worth asking whether it may be possible for architectural education to incorporate new bodies of research-based theory and technique while retaining the traditions of the studio as the heart of its curriculum. This would require an expansion of the range of design domains taken as pertinent to studio practice. Students engaged in the traditional learning-by-doing of project-based studio education would also be exposed to specialized fields of knowledge taken to be useful for design, and exposed in such a way that they can bring that knowledge to bear on their studio projects. How best to do this is a problem, though not a new one. It has already arisen in

86

connection with such special fields as lighting, acoustics, soil mechanics, and structural engineering. It may be addressed by creating specialized studios that focus on particular technical problems within a larger design context, by organizing studio projects around student teams that include technical specialists, or by mounting specialized courses or tutorials in the intervals between, or around, studios. As the newer fields proliferate, however, they tend to threaten the studio's special status. Architectural education may begin to look less like itself and more like the normative curriculum of the other university-based professional schools. How, then, might the newer fields of specialized knowledge enter into the studio experience?

The perspective on designing that I have proposed suggests at least a partial answer to this question. If we see designing as reflection-in-action — that is, as a kind of on-the-spot research process, conducted in media and according to standards of rigor special to architecture — then we can also see how new technical fields may be incorporated into architectural education, by exposing students not primarily to their results but to make their methods of inquiry. Two existing examples come to mind. At the University of Southern California, Ralph Knowles has designed studios in which students carry out research on the limits and potentials of the "solar envelope", exploring systematically how the design of groups of buildings would be constrained by strict observance of the "sun rights" of their own and neighbouring users. And at Harvard Graduate School of Design, environmental design students of Richard Kraus have done masters theses in which, as part of a design project, they explore and experiment with phenomena such as the semi-enclosed spaces of an urban area, on the "wedges" by which one neighborhood penetrates another. Research, in the sense illustrated by these examples, consists in extending the on-the-spot experimentation peculiar to designing to include phenomena and methods of inquiry often excluded from design. Rather than learning only to use the results of a special discipline in his designing, the student learns to do in the course of his designing a version of the sort of research represented by that discipline. He has a chance to gain acquaintance with an applied science, not only as a body of knowledge to be drawn upon, but as a way of inquiring capable of integration with his own reflection-in-action.

A similar approach may be taken to the increasingly important question of the role of the computer in design practice and education. Some architects see the computer as a technology incompatible with the preferred image of architecture as an art. Others, enamored of the "expert system" of artificial intelligence, see it as a potential executor of design tasks. Still others envisage a computational environment for design, a tool that would enhance the designer's capacity by giving him, at his fingertips, a field of relevant information about the contexts and consequences of design decisions far in excess of the ordinary designer's store of remembered knowledge. But it is also possible to see the computer as an environment for experimentation. On this view, the designer would employ the computer to generate graphic representations of spaces and simulate design moves and consequences with a high degree of precision and complexity. He could, for example — as some researchers at the Massachusetts Institute of Technology are now doing — explore the capacity of various spatial configurations to carry particular architectural programs. Programs are being devised which may enable the designer to play out, more systematically and rigorously than before, the web of moves, consequences and implications that follows from a particular set of design premises and values. In dialogue with a computer programmed for this role, a student might explore the adequacy of his attempts to describe the understandings that inform his own design practice.

What other professions can learn from the architectural studio

Not only students of design, but all those who seek to learn the artistry of a practise new to them, face an epistemological paradox and psychological predicament. They need to educate themselves to a new competence when they don't yet know what it is they need to learn. And they must therefore take a plunge into *doing* before they know what to do. Similarly, those who try to help these students need an artistry of coaching, similar in its essentials to the artistry they want to help their students acquire.

Coaching artistry flourishes in a setting like the architectural studio with its physical arrangements for doing and making things, its patterns of organization, and its cultural traditions. The creation of such a setting serves to punctuate the otherwise amorphous and unlimited doing in which students and coaches need to be engaged, gives a more or less predictable framework for the interactions of students and studio masters, and institutionalizes expectations about peformance, demonstration, imitation and criticism.

The generalized setting for learning-by-doing, of which the architectural studio is an exemplar, I shall call a *reflective practicum*. It differs in several important ways from the clinics, laboratories, field experiences, and workshops that play the role of practicum in many of the professional schools. A reflective practicum would not be organized to apply classroom knowledge to practical problems. It would be studio-like in the sense that it would organize itself around projects of simulated practice and would ask students to plunge into these before they know what they need to be doing or learning. It would expose students to the demonstrations, advice, and criticism of master practitioners. It would focus on the messiness of problematic situations which need to be converted to well-formed problems before they can be solved by the application of established techniques. It would pay attention to the strangeness of unique cases that escape the categories of established theories. And it would engage the appreciative, value-laden questions as well as the technical ones. It would not eschew the use of research-based knowledge, but it would not assume that project tasks are only done, or best done, through the use of such knowledge.

In fact, some of the existing practicums of the professional schools fit the description I have so far given. The problem is that, according to the prevailing norms of the schools, they are not supposed to do so. It is not uncommon to find medical students in the clinic, engineers in the laboratory, or social workers in the field, who discover that, although they are learning something important, it is not what the school seems to assume they are learning. They are not "applying" what they have already learned in the classroom but are acquiring, instead, a different order of knowing-in-action through exposure to the demonstrations, advice, and criticism of their clinical instructors and their peers. It does not help matters that the clinical instructors are often lower in status than their classroom professors in the disciplines judged relevant to practice.

Indeed, it is just this "dual curriculum" — that quality of presuming to do one thing while actually doing another — that makes the practicum problematic, difficult to teach, and an opening for the wedge of education reform. The practicum is the place where incongruity, between the school's formulation

89

of professional knowledge and the knowing-in-action implicit in competent practice, comes sharply into focus.

A reflective practicum, as I mean it, would go beyond the description I have given above in that it would make the relations between these two kinds of knowledge a matter of explicit inquiry. It would not assume that we can know in advance what bodies of theory and technique may prove useful a particular case. Emphasis would be placed on the theories implicit in the practice of the master practitioner and on the effort to make these accessible to the student, as well as on the student's development of the capacity to invent and test theories *ad hoc* in the practice situation.

In a reflective practicum, it is assumed that both instructor and student know more than they can say. The instructor seeks to reflect aloud on the reflection-in-action implicit in her demonstrations, and on the assumptional basis of her judgments of the student's work. The student is encouraged to reflect on what he already knows, on the difficulties he experiences, and on the emergent understanding implicit in his performances. The instructor is called upon to display a coach's artistry, a capacity for reflection-in-action on the task of figuring out how what is to be learned can best be linked to a student's present understandings and difficulties. The instructor must be able to generate multiple representations of substantive knowledge and know-how, and shift easily from one representation to another. She must be able to function as on-the-spot researcher into the student's understanding of the phenomena, and have on the tip of her tongue — or be able to invent — a method suited to this particular student. In communicative transactions with the student, she must be able to move up and down the ladder of reflection. She must continually ask herself, "What are they making of this?" And she must do all of this in such a way as to minimize her responsibility for triggering the student's defenses.

The reflective practicum should function as the core of the larger professional curriculum. Relevant applied science and technique should be taught in close proximity to project activity, and should take the forms most immediately useful to practice — that is, on the one hand, as a *repertoire* of potentially useful examples, canonical problems, images, metaphors and rules of thumb and, on the other hand, as a way of seeing and inquiring that can be employed in the practice situation.

Town planners should be expected, for example, to know about real estate markets, population movements, determinants of the uses of public spaces. Physicians should undoubtedly learn biology, anatomy, and the physiology of disease; public administrators, organizational theory and economics; teachers, cognitive and developmental psychology. But aspiring practitioners need to learn such disciplines in a form most congenial to practice — which does not, I think, mean a watered-down version of the way in which they are taught to discipline-based researchers. Usable knowledge often takes the form of examples of knowledge in action, in terms of which the practitioner can then see the next similar situation. A working planner can profit from a richly developed example of the way in which an economist looks at the meaning of a property tax increase. A public administrator, armed with descriptions of power games draped over bureaucratic structures, can learn to see his own organization in those terms. Practitioners need to build up a "library of the mind", each element of which contains a *use* of a theoretical perspective to make sense of a practice situation.

Further, the sciences judged relevant to practice should be taught as exemplars of a kind of inquiry, aiming primarily at helping students invent and test theories *ad hoc* in the practice situation and only secondarily at informing them about the results of research in the field. Consider, for example, the ways in which Piaget's theories of cognitive development may be brought to bear on the education of teachers. On this point Piaget himself was extraordinarily modest; he carefully refrained from any claim to practical utility. Some of Piaget's readers and followers, however, have advocated a pedagogy based on the famous stages of cognitive development. They have claimed, variously, that educational content should be geared to the stages of development of the child in question — or, on the contrary, that teachers should aim at accelerating the child's passage through the stages of development. Both approaches are of dubious efficacy. In contrast, some neo-Piagetians have thought in terms of a practice of teacher-education which would encourage teachers to *be* Piaget — that is, to learn to become effective on-line researchers into the understandings revealed in learning situations by the child's words and actions. For this purpose, students need to be initiated into a research process. They need not only the sorts of presentations of research ordinarily found in scientific journals and texts, but accounts of the inquiry that produced those results. They need exposure to just what tends to be left out of journals and texts.

This proposal has direct bearing on the dilemma of rigor or relevance. Theories and techniques literally applicable only on the high, hard ground may be useful, nevertheless, in the swamp below — not as rules for application but as examples of a kind of inquiry to be approximated in the relatively uncontrolled situations of practice. When the artistry of practice is seen as a kind of research, then the preliminary groping and experimentation of the laboratory scientist can function as exemplars, like and unlike the explorations and on-the-spot experiments of competent practitioners in the indeterminate zones of practice. It is only when science is seen after-the-fact, as a set of elegant research results, that it seems hopelessly distant from the artistry that some individuals bring to their lives in the swamp.

Finally, the idea of a studio-like reflective practicum has implications for the kinds of research proper to professional schools. The most important source of useful professional knowledge, in the sense I propose, is the practice of competent practitioners. In part, this can become available to students through the reflective practicum. But there is also a need for systematic observation of and reflection on the knowledge built into competent practice in the field, including the dilemmas and dead-ends encountered there and what practitioners do with them. One should also include attention to the ways in which the artistry of problem-setting clears the ground for technical problem-solving and the ways in which reflection-in-action mediates the uses of research-based theory in practice. Research of this kind would require collaboration between researchers and practitioners. Practitioners would function here as co-researchers into their own practice — an activity that can and should be combined with continuing education.

Architecture as a form of higher education	In such countries as France and Italy, in Mexico and in other Latin American countries, tens of thousands of university students enroll in schools of architecture, not as preparation for a professional career in architecture, but as a form of general higher education. They study architecture as they might study history, economics, or philosophy, and as generations of British students studied classics, to gain a general background from

which to go on to careers in business or government service. For them, the study of architecture serves as an alternative form of education in the liberal arts. In the United Kingdom and the United States, many students of architecture go on to take degrees in other fields, and many who graduate with degrees in architecture do not go on to practice. For these students, architecture functions in fact as a form of general or liberal arts education, whatever its espoused or intended function may be.

At a time of debate in academic and governmental circles over the future of the schools of architecture — a debate fuelled by claims of an oversupply of graduates in relation to the demand for practitioners — it is important to consider the implications of adopting as a matter of policy what has tended to happen willy-nilly as a matter of fact. What special contributions does the study of architecture bring to higher education? And what would follow if schools of architecture were to make a more deliberate claim to a role in general liberal arts education?

It is important to distinguish the educational uses of the study of architecture from the educational uses of involvement in architectural design. As a field of study, architecture can be seen as a medium of cultural expression. We study the art of architecture, as we might study literature, dance, or the visual arts, from the point of view of appreciation and criticism. Architecture is also a hybrid field, a combination of arts and technics, and the configurations of the built environment can be studied as expressions of social purposes and aspirations, of cultural and technological patterns. So we can describe and analyse the evolution of the form of the house in interaction with technologies of temperature control. We can study the languages of architectural design, learning to "read" buildings as others "read" the artefacts or written texts produced by a culture. We can study, as Henri Focillon did, the architectural forms of the romanesque and Gothic cathedrals as evidence of interactions of religious sensibility and building technology, and as an evolving "life of forms" in the environment of artefacts. These and other family-resembling studies lie well within the traditions of liberal arts education, in whose currently embattled domains (at least in the United States) architecture is probably no better or worse off than other intellectual pursuits conventionally described as liberal arts.

93

When we consider the architectural studio as a special feature of architecture's contribution to higher education, however, we come up against a very different sort of phenomenon. Studio education is education in *making* things — namely, the representations of things to be built. It is not only or primarily about appreciation, or criticism, or analysis of the relations of variables drawn from the study of natural or man-made worlds. It is a form of education in making in the sense of involvement with concrete materials, shaping them in relation to a vision of desirable outcomes. It is bound up with sketch pads, tracing paper, and scale models. It begins with problematic situations, in which there are initially more variables than one can handle — often, where one does not know the names of the relevant variables — and it involves an attempt to construct an understandable coherence through moves which can never have only the effects anticipated for them. Materials "talk back", when the maker is prepared to listen, provoking a reinterpretation of results and a reframing of the vision to be realized or the problem to be solved. All of this is evident in the characteristic environment of the studio, with its odd (to the non-architect) combination of messiness and order. In a place like the Massachusetts Institute of Technology, where I teach, a casual walk from office to classroom, passing by computer rooms, laboratories and architectural lofts, is enough to suggest the uniqueness of the studio environment.

Conceived as a kind of making, architectural designing is practical; it may employ studies, but it is primarily engaged in doing. It is synthetic, in the sense of putting together kinds of things and kinds of knowledge. It requires a combination of artistry, with its feel for materials, together with usable understandings of applied science and technology. It is also normative, insofar as it depends on appreciations, involves vision-construction, and demands an ethic for the design process.

The architectural studio is one of the few forms of traditional higher education centred on making things. (Even engineering education, which in the years prior to World War II was bound to the manipulation of particular pieces of equipment, has since the late 1950's strenuously sought to reconstitute itself as the study of engineering science.) Lately, this fact has taken on a new meaning. Since the 1960's, it is not only professional education, as I have already shown, but higher education as a

94

whole that has been criticized for its disjunction from the world
of practice. Critics of the universities — students and professors
among them — have inveighed against the academy's tendency
to divorce theory from practice and analysis from action. More
recently, as tuition fees have risen and students have become
more concentrated on the wish to prepare for employment, the
calls for "relevance" have become more strident, as has the
academic backlash against vocationalism. Not a few institutions
have frankly embraced pre-vocational, or pre-professional,
programs. Others have gone to considerable lengths to make
the liberal arts more palatable to students with jobs in mind.

At the same time, there are signs of a growning intellectual
interest in the process of design, or making, as a powerful
metaphor for activities usually conceived in other ways.
Herbert Simon, in his *The Sciences of the Artificial,* asserts
boldly that, "Everyone designs who devises courses of action
aimed at changing existing situations into preferred ones".[1] He
construes design, in this sense, as "the core of all professional
training . . . the principal mark that distinguishes the
professions from the sciences".[2] But he goes on to argue that,
in their "hankering after academic respectability",[3] professional
schools have "abdicated responsibility for training in the core
professional skill".[4] He concludes that:

> . . . professional schools will reassume their professional
> responsibilities just to the degree that they can discover a
> science of design, a body of intellectually tough, analytic,
> partly formalizable, partly empirical, teachable doctrine
> about the design process.[5]

Russell Ackoff, who began his remarkable career as an
architect and proceeded through philosophy of science to
operations research and management, has argued, in *Creating
the Corporate future,* for a reconceptualization of organizational
planning and management as a process of design — one in
which the practitioner makes his desired future,

> The selection of ideals lies at the very core of interactive
> planning; it takes place through *idealized design* of a system
> that does not exist, or *idealized redesign* of one that does.
> Such a design or redesign is a conception of the system that
> its designers would like to have a *right now,* not at some
> future date.[6]

Designing is at the heart of Ackoff's theory of planning as it is
at the heart of his continuing practice.

Indeed, among some philosophers there are efforts to reconceptualize scientific, analytic, and theoretical activities in terms of the metaphor of making. Perhaps the most compelling of these is Nelson Goodman's *Ways of World-Making,* in which the noted analytic philosopher argues for a "constructionalist" view of perception and knowledge. In acts of perception, appreciation and creation, as in the act of theory-building, he claims, we construct the worlds we inhabit and live in multiple actual worlds of our own making. Thus, "the arts must be taken no less seriously than the sciences as modes of discovery, creation, and enlargement of knowledge in the broad sense of advancement of the understanding . . ."[7] And,

> Even if the ultimate product of science, unlike that of art, is a literal, verbal, or mathematical, denotational theory, science and art proceed in much the same way with their searching and building.[8]

All of this suggests a growing readiness to see making and designing as central to the intellectual as to the practical life, and therefore to higer education — not only in response to criticism of the academy's divergence from the world of practice but as a consequence of the recognition of making as a powerful metaphor for intelligent action in domains long thought to be remote from the shaping of concrete materials for human ends.

It would be unfortunate, in view of this emerging readiness to see and appreciate the unique features of architectural education, if university or government officials were to respond to budgetary pressures by treating schools of architecture as vulnerable targets of opportunity. It would be even worse if they were to use budgetary constraints as an excuse from trimming off what seemed to them to be marginal accretions on the body of the university. For, perhaps more than any other existing branch, architecture offers clues to the reform and revitalization of higher education.

On the other hand, if schools of architecture bid for wider legitimization of their alternative role as providers of general higher education, they must take on a commitment to explore and develop their connections to other forms of intelligent activity, and therefore, to other branches of learning. We have already considered architecture's relation to applied science and technology. But in at least two other directions, architecture should be searching out new connections.

If architecture is the prototypical design activity, its more generic role in higher education would be enhanced by examination of its relationships to other modes of designing — not only in the design professions but in the other arts, and in callings not usually framed in terms of design. If architects wish to stop short of Herbert Simon's proposal for a universal science of design, they may nevertheless find it profitable to explore their family resemblances to, and differences from, kinds of designing undertaken in different media and with different ends in view.

Architecture is a normative discipline, concerned with preferences, ideals, commitments and obligations. The work of the architectural studio is also normative, engaging students in the task of imagining desirable places and spaces, not only in constructing them and in setting design problems worth solving. There are other normative disciplines — philosophy, economics, engineering, history, the study of literature, among them. How might the architectural studio frankly embracing its role in general education, draw on such disciplines as these to enrich the problem-setting dimensions of studio practice?

These lines of inquiry seem to me essential, if schools of architecture are to move from their present position at the margins of higher education to a position of educational leadership. It would not be the first time that leadership will have come from the margins. But any such movement is very likely to bring with it a transformation of the mover. To the extent that schools of architecture take one or more of these directions — responding to the challenges of a shifting context of architectural practice, presenting themselves as an exemplar for professional education, bidding more deliberately and forcefully for a role in higher education — they will need to reflect on the essential features of their studio traditions. For, as they incorporate new elements that hold great potential for change, they will need to be more aware than heretofore of the norms and practices they wish to hold constant.

Notes

1. Informal communication, Dean Edward Anderson, MIT, 1983.
2. *Ibid.*
3. See *The Reflective Practitioner*, Donald A. Schön, Basic Books, January, 1983; summarized, in part, in Part I, to follow.
4. Nathan Glazer, "The Schools of the Minor Professions", *Minerva*, 1974; 346.
5. Edgar Schein, *Professional Education*, McGraw Hill, 1973; 43.
6. Herbert Simon, *The Sciences of the Artificial*, MIT Press, 1976, Cambridge, Massachusetts.
7. See *Study of Architectural Education*, MIT, 1982, edited by W. Porter and M. Kilbridge, Report to the Andrew Mellon Foundation, as an example of a more comprehensive study.

Part I: Dilemmas of Contemporary Professional Education

1. Everett Hughes, "The Study of Occupations", in Merton and Broom, *eds., Sociology Today*, Basic Books, New York, 1959.
2. Kenneth Lynn, Introduction to "The Professions", Fall, 1963, issue of *Daedalus, Journal of the American Academy of Arts and Sciences*, p. 649.
3. James Gustafson, "The Clergy in the United States", in *Daedalus, op. cit.*, p. 743.
4. William Alonso, "Cities and City Planners", in *Daedalus, op. cit.*, p. 838.
5. Edgar Schein, *Professional Education*, McGraw Hill, New York, p. 43.
6. Nathan Glazer, "The Schools of the Minor Professions", in *Minerva*, Vol. XII, No. 3, July, 1974.
7. *Ibid.*, p. 363.
8. *Ibid.*, p. 363.
9. For a discussion of Positivism and its influence on prevailing epistemological views, see Jergen Habermas, *Knowledge and Human Interests*, Beacon Press, Boston, Massachusetts, 1968. And for a discussion of the influence of Positivist doctrines on the shaping of the modern university, see Edward Shils, "The Order of Learning in the United States from 1865 to 1920: The Ascendancy of the Universities", *Minerva*, Vol. XVI, No. 2, Summer, 1978.
10. Thorsten Veblen, *The Higher Learning in America*, Reprint of the 1918 edition, Kelley, New York.
11. I have taken this term from Herbert Simon, who gives a particularly useful example of a well-formed problem in his *The Science of the Artificial*, MIT Press, Cambridge, Mass., 1972.
12. Martin Rein and I have written about problem-setting in "Problem-Setting in Policy Research", in Carol Weiss, ed., *Using Social Research in Public Policy Making*, D.C. Heath, Lexington, Mass., 1977.
13. For an example of multiple views of the malnourishment problem, see Berg, Scrimshaw and Call, *eds., Nutrition, National Development, and Planning*, MIT Press, Cambridge, Mass., 1973.
14. See Russell Ackoff, "The Future of Operational Research is Past", *Journal of Operational Research Soc.*, Vol. 30, No. 2, pp. 93-104, Pergamon Press Ltd., 1979.
15. I have taken this phrase from the work of the psychiatrist, Harry Stack Sullivan.
16. The term is Clifford Geertz's. See his *The Interpretation of Cultures*, Selected Essays by Clifford Geertz, Basic Books, New York, 1973.
17. Schein, *op. cit.*, p. 44.

18. As Richard Bernstein has written (*The Restructuring of Social and Political Theory*, Harcourt, Brace, Jovanovich, New York, 1976), "There is not a single major thesis advanced by either nineteen century Positivists or the Vienna Circle that has not been devastatingly criticized when measured by the Positivists' own standards for philosophical argument. The original formulations of the analytic-synthetic dichotomy and the verifiability criterion on meaning have been abandoned. It has been effectively shown that the Positivists' understanding of the natural sciences and the formal disciplines is grossly oversimplified. Whatever one's final judgment about the current disputes in the post-empiricist philosophy and history of science . . . there is rational agreement about the inadequacy of the original Positivist understanding of science, knowledge, and meaning.

Part II: Reflection-in-Action
1. Gilbert Ryle, "On Knowing How and Knowing That", in *The Concept of Mind*, Hutcheson, London, 1949, p. 32.
2. Andrew Harrison, *Making and Thinking*, Hacket, Indianapolis, 1978.
3. Michael Polany, *The Tacit Dimension*, Doubleday and Co., New York, 1967, p. 12.
4. Chris Alexander, *Notes Toward the Synthesis of Forum*, Harvard University Press, Cambridge, Mass., 1964.
5. Geoffrey Vickers, unpublished memorandum, MIT, 1978.
6. Chester Barnard, *The Functions of the Executive*, Harvard University Press, Cambridge, Mass., 1968, p. 306; first published in 1938.

Part III: The Architectural Studio
1. Material for this chapter was drawn from the work of Roger Simmonds, he collected the protocol I have used here, although he is not responsible for my analysis of it. Simmonds' doctoral thesis in the School of Architecture and Planning at MIT explores the experience of the larger studio of which "Quist" and "Petra" — fictional names of real participants — were part.
   This chapter includes, in summarized and somewhat different from, material from my book, *The Reflective Practitioner*, Basic Books, 1983.

Part IV: The Paradox and Predicament of Learning to Design
1. This example, and its quotations, are drawn from a case study of a design studio made by Florian van Buttlar, MIT, Study of Architectural Education, 1981.
2. *Ibid.*
3. *Plato: Protagoras and Meno*, translated by W.K.C. Guthrie, Penguin Books, 1972; 128.
4. Thomas Cowan, informal communication to the author.
5. See Michael Reedy, "The Conduit Metaphor", in A. Ortony, *ed.*, *Metaphor and Thought*, Cambridge University Press, Cambridge, England, 1979.

Part V: Coaching Artistry
1. Leo Tolstoy, "On Teaching the Rudiments", in *Tolstoy on Education*, Leo Wiener, *ed.*, University of Chicago Press, Chicago, IL, 1967; 58.

Part VI: Conclusion
1. Simon, *Ibid.*, p. 55.
2. *Ibid.*, p. 56.
3. *Ibid.*, p. 56.
4. *Ibid.*, p. 57.
5. *Ibid.*, p. 58.
6. Russell L. Ackoff, *Creating the Corporate Future*, John Wiley and Sons, New York, 1981; 105.
7. Nelson Goodman, *Ways of Worldmaking*, Hackett Publishing Company, 1978; 102.
8. *Ibid.*, p. 107.